Expressive Writing

Words that Heal

James W. Pennebaker, Ph.D.
Professor of Psychology
The University of Texas at Austin

and

John F. Evans, Ed.D.
Integrative Health Coach
Wellness & Writing Connections

Idyll Arbor, Inc.

39129 264th Ave SE, Enumclaw, WA 98022 (360) 825-7797

Idyll Arbor, Inc. Editor: JoAnne Dyer
ISBN 9781611580464 paper
ISBN 9781611580471 ebook

Correspondence should be sent to
James Pennebaker, Department of Psychology A8000, The University of Texas, Austin, TX 78712 (email: Pennebaker@mail.utexas.edu)
or
John Evans, Wellness & Writing Connections, 1516 Great Ridge Parkway, Chapel Hill, NC 27516 (email: info@wellnessandwritingconnections.com)

Library of Congress Cataloging-in-Publication Data
Pennebaker, James W.
  Expressive writing : words that heal / James W. Pennebaker, Ph.D., professor of psychology, The University of Texas at Austin, and John F. Evans, Ed.D., integrative health coach, Wellness & Writing Connections.
       pages cm
  Includes bibliographical references.
  ISBN 978-1-61158-046-4 (trade paper) -- ISBN 978-1-61158-047-1 (e-book)
  1. Diaries--Therapeutic use. 2. Diaries--Authorship--Psychological aspects. 3. Writing--Psychological aspects. I. Evans, John Frank. II. Title. III. Title: Words that heal.
  RC489.D5P46 2014
  616.89'1656--dc23
                                                                    2013050169

Contents

Authors' Prefaces v

I. The Essentials of Writing for Health 1

    1. Why Write about Trauma or Emotional Upheaval? 3

    2. How Can We Get Ready To Write? 22

    3. What Are the Basic Writing Techniques? 31

    4. How Can We Look Back at Our Writing? 42

II. Experimenting with Writing 53

    5. Writing to Break Mental Blocks 55

    6. Writing to Appreciate the Good in a Sometimes Bad World 60

    7. Writing and Editing Your Story 67

    8. Writing to Change Perspectives 75

    9. Writing in Different Contexts 84

    10. Writing Creatively with Fiction, Poetry, Dance, and Art 94

III. Transform Your Health: Writing to Heal 105

    11. Expressive Writing 107

    12. Transactional Writing 122

    13. Poetic Writing 129

    14. Story Telling 140

    15. Affirmative Writing 158

    16. Legacy Writing 164

    17. Conclusions 169

    Resources 171

    Reading List 175

    References and Additional Scientific Readings 177

Authors' Prefaces

"Writing saved my life." From best-selling authors to private journal keepers, from students entering college to soldiers returning home after deployment, from those who recently lost a loved one to those who suffer from childhood violence, we hear how writing saves lives. I've said the same thing myself.

Writing has helped me deal with my own health challenges, including PTSD, a diagnosis of advanced cancer, and a recent cancer recurrence. In fact, this book might not exist had I not come across the first edition of James Pennebaker's *Writing to Heal* ten years ago. Learning about personal and expressive writing helped me regain my health and live a more happy and productive life.

When *Writing to Heal* was published in 2004, it was the first journaling book that was rooted firmly in scientific research. What drew me to it was my own need for healing, my hope that after all my years of teaching and studying academic writing that I might find something that would allow me to write my way out of a serious depression.

After reading just a few pages, I discovered why my own writing hadn't been helping me. I was stuck in a never-ending cycle of rumination — telling the same story over and over. There was no arc in my story; it was a flat line. Then when my story arc turned starkly downward, I knew it was killing me from the inside. *Writing to Heal* explained why I needed to write a new story in a new way.

Pennebaker's book provided me a way to work out the most troubling events in my life, but in a way I had never done before. The writing assignments provided a life-course correction by helping me bring closure to painful childhood memories, recall experiences from my youth with a more positive perspective, and get beyond the emotional turmoil from my own adult mistakes.

Writing to Heal also opened up new professional interests and opportunities. I began to work with a local therapist to lead her clients in writing to heal group sessions. As my writing to heal practice grew, so did my desire to bring other like-minded professionals together. In 2007, I created Wellness & Writing Connections, LLC and the Wellness & Writing Connections Conference series so counselors, healthcare professionals, educators, and others could share how they were using writing with their clients, patients, and students.

Over the next four years, several hundred healthcare professionals, counselors, educators, and others interested in writing to heal came together at the Wellness & Writing Connections Conferences in Atlanta. Studying over a hundred concurrent conference sessions, I identified guiding principles and defining characteristics in the types of exercises presented at the conferences. From these findings and from studying my clients' responses in workshops and clinical settings, I developed several writing to heal programs, like Transform Your Health: Write to Heal in Part III of this book.

Through all of this, I developed an easy friendship with James Pennebaker, or Jamie, as he likes to be called. When Jamie and I gave a talk and workshop on Writing to Heal at Duke Integrative Medicine in March 2012, I learned that *Writing to Heal* was out of print. I offered to help update, revise, and enlarge it so it could be available again. Jamie agreed and we made plans to collaborate on this project.

This book is the result of our collaboration. We agree that it brings together clinical and scientific perspectives that can help people learn more about the process of writing and move towards better health — physically and emotionally.

John F. Evans
Chapel Hill, NC

If you are currently living with a trauma or emotional upheaval, you have made a courageous step by opening this book. You may be seeking a way to deal with this event so that you can get on with your life. It's tempting to avoid thinking about the trauma altogether and pretend that everything is fine. Some of your closest friends might want you to do this as well. In reality, though, you can't ignore a massive upheaval that is probably affecting every part of your life.

This book was written for people living with a trauma or an emotional upheaval. It may have occurred in the distant past, or you may be in the middle of it right now. It could be a single event or a long-term chronic problem. Whatever it is, you probably find yourself thinking, worrying, even dreaming about it far too much. Hopefully, some form of expressive writing, as described in this book, can help you get through some of the conflict, stress, or pain that you are feeling.

Dozens of workbooks, workshops, and self-help systems are available to help you deal with emotional upheavals. Some may be beneficial for you; others may not. Most have been developed by people who work with clients on a day-to-day basis. I'm not one of those people. I'm a research psychologist who accidentally discovered the power of writing in an experiment I conducted in the mid-1980s. In the study, people were asked to write for four consecutive days, fifteen minutes per day, about either a traumatic experience or a superficial event. To my surprise, those who wrote about traumas went to the doctor less often in the following months, and many said their writing changed their lives. Ever since then, I've been devoted to understanding the mysteries of emotional writing.

Since the original publication of *Writing to Heal*, I have spoken with hundreds of people who have used expressive writing or other forms of journaling to improve their lives. In these discussions, I realized that I needed the advice of someone who had far more practical clinical experience than I had. I was fortunate to have met John Evans, who was just such a person. Through our discussions, it occurred to me that he would be a perfect co-author on this revision of the earlier book.

What we have tried to do in this book is to maintain the scientific integrity of the work while at the same time offering concrete recommendations for ways to cope with emotional upheavals. The book is written in three parts. The first focuses on the background of writing and basic techniques we know to be helpful. The second is more experimental. The goal of that part is for you to try out new writing methods that may be helpful. Some might work wonderfully; others might not help at all. The final section of the book was inspired by John and reflects his deep commitment to writing and physical health. In this section, we introduce a more structured approach to writing in ways that improve your physical and mental health.

I recommend you start by following the writing instructions outlined in Chapter 3. If you feel that the traditional writing exercise is beneficial, that's great. If not, try other techniques discussed in later chapters. Be responsible for figuring out the best way to tackle your own demons. For example, some people like to write and then throw away their writing. Others prefer to write, then rewrite, and then rewrite their story again and again, editing and altering the story over time.

There is no absolute answer or correct way to write or to get past an emotional upheaval. Use this book as a rough guide. Stick with what works — and drop what doesn't. Above all, trust your own intuition to know if you are going in the right direction.

James W. Pennebaker
Austin, Texas

PART I

The Essentials of Writing for Health

The unexamined life is not worth living.

— Socrates

Part I looks at the basics of Expressive Writing. We include some of the scientific studies that support the use of writing, how to get ready to write, the writing techniques, and how we can learn from what we have written. Part I was written by Jamie Pennebaker and is based on his research since the 1980s.

1

Why Write about Trauma or Emotional Upheaval?

What is the best way to get past a trauma, improve health, and build resilience? Researchers have been tackling this question in many ways over the last century. In-depth psychotherapy and medication have helped millions of people. Relaxation techniques including yoga and meditation have also proven beneficial. Strenuous exercise and improved eating habits can also help. Unfortunately, sometimes none of these techniques work. The best we can say is that some of these strategies work for some people, some of the time. There is no guaranteed technique.

The purpose of this chapter is to convince you that writing is a potentially effective method to deal with traumas or other emotional upheavals. The research evidence is indeed promising.

Since the mid-1980s, an increasing number of studies have focused on expressive writing as a way to bring about healing. The first studies indicated that writing about traumatic experiences for as little as twenty minutes a day for three or four days can produce measurable changes in people's physical and mental health. More recent studies demonstrate that just one day can provide healthful benefits (Chung & Pennebaker 2008). Emotional writing — or what is often described in research studies as Expressive Writing (EW) — can positively affect people's sleeping habits, work efficiency, and their connections to others. Indeed, when we put traumatic experiences into words, we tend to be less concerned with the emotional events that have been weighing us down.

Perhaps you don't need convincing, or you aren't interested in the scientific research about writing. If you want to skip the research and logic behind expressive writing and are ready to jump in and try it, go directly to Chapter 2 for a four-day writing experience. Or skip even further ahead to Part III to try your hand at a six-week program of sequential writing exercises. However you choose to use this book is up to you.

If, like me, you are a bit skeptical of any new method that purports to help people cope with traumatic experience, read on. It may be helpful for you to learn how expressive writing has been tested, when and with whom it works, and when it has not produced compelling results.

Emotional Writing: A Brief History

At the outset, it's only fair to warn you that I am not a completely objective source about the power of writing. I'm a researcher, not a therapist. In the late 1970s and early 1980s, I investigated traumatic experiences of all types: deaths of spouses, natural disasters, sexual traumas of all sorts, divorce, physical abuse, the Holocaust.

The scientific community had known for years that any kind of trauma was highly stressful. After an emotional upheaval, people were likely to become depressed, get sick, gain or lose weight, and even die from heart disease and cancer at higher rates. In fact, a landmark study (the Adverse Childhood Experiences Study) of over 12,000 people established that trauma in childhood was a strong predictor of serious illness in adulthood (Stockdale 2011; Brown et al. 2010; Dube et al. 2009; Fellitti 2009.) When my students and I studied the aftereffects of traumas, we observed the same things these researchers did.

But we also found something more striking. Having a traumatic experience was certainly bad for people in many ways, but people who had a trauma and kept that traumatic experience secret were much worse off. Not talking to others about a trauma, we learned, placed people at even higher risk for major and minor illness compared to people who did talk about their traumas.

The dangers of keeping secrets were most apparent for major life traumas. In a series of surveys, several hundred college students and people who worked at a large corporation were asked to complete a brief questionnaire about traumas that had occurred earlier in their lives. The respondents were asked if prior to the age of seventeen they had experienced the death of a family member, the divorce of parents, a sexual trauma, physical abuse, or some other event that had "changed their personality." For each item, they were also queried as to whether they had talked to anyone in detail about this experience.

Three of the striking results are apparent in Figure 1. First, over half of the people we surveyed reported having experienced a major trauma in their life prior to the age of seventeen. (Keep in mind that these were generally middle and upper-middle class students and adults.) Second, the people who had had any kind of major trauma before age of

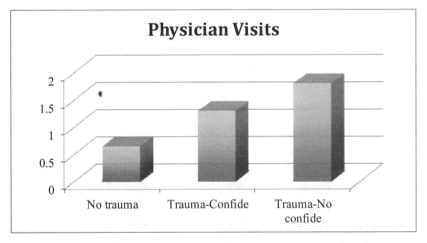

Figure 1. Yearly physician visits for illness among people who report not having had a childhood trauma (No Trauma), having had one or more traumas about which they confided (Trauma — Confide), or having had at least one significant childhood trauma that they had kept secret (Trauma — No Confide).

seventeen went to physicians for illness at twice the rate of people who had not had a trauma. Finally, among those who had traumas, those who kept their traumas secret went to physicians almost forty percent more often than those who openly talked about their traumas (Pennebaker & Susman 1988).

Later research projects from multiple labs confirmed these results. Adults whose spouses had committed suicide or died suddenly in car accidents were healthier in the year following the death if they talked about the trauma than if they didn't talk about it. Gays and lesbians who openly disclosed their sexual status — that is, were out of the closet — were found to have fewer major health problems than if they kept their orientation secret (Cole, Kemeny, Taylor, et al. 1996). Not talking about important issues in your life poses a significant health risk.

These original findings about secrets led to the first writing study. If not talking was potentially unhealthy, would asking people to talk — or even write — about emotional upheavals produce health improvements? In the mid-1980s, we tested this idea directly.

Almost fifty students participated in the first writing project. They were regular young adults who were reasonably healthy; most had just started college. When they signed up for the experiment, they knew that they would be writing for fifteen minutes per day for four consecutive days. The only thing they didn't know was what their writing topics would be. By the flip of a coin, students were asked to write about emotional, traumatic topics or about superficial, non-emotional topics.

Because this turned out to be a life-changing experiment for some of the participants (as well as for me), it may be helpful for you to imagine what it was like for the people who were asked to write about emotional topics. Imagine that you were escorted into my office and you were told the following:

You have signed up for an experiment where you will be writing for four days, fifteen minutes per day in a solitary room down the hall. Everything you write will be completely anonymous and confidential. You will never receive any feedback about your writing. At the conclusion of each day's writing, we ask that you put your writing in a large box so that we can analyze it. However, your giving it to us is completely up to you.

In your writing, I want you to really let go and explore your very deepest thoughts and feelings about the most traumatic experience of your life. In your writing, try to tie this traumatic experience to other parts of your life — your childhood, your relationship with your parents, close friends, lovers, or others important to you. You might link your writing to your future and who you would like to become, to who you have been in the past, or to who you are now. The important thing is that you really let go and write about your deepest emotions and thoughts. You can write about the same thing for all four days or about different things on each day — that is entirely up to you. Many people have not had traumatic experiences, but all of us have faced major conflicts or stressors — and you can write about those as well.

Many students were stunned by these instructions. To our surprise, no one had ever encouraged them to write about some of the most significant experiences of their lives. Nevertheless, they went into their cubicles and wrote their hearts out. In this study, as in every study I have run, people wrote about truly horrible experiences in their lives — terrible divorce stories, rape, physical abuse in the family, suicide attempts, and even quirky things that could never be categorized. Many students came out of their writing rooms in tears. Clearly, the experiment was an emotionally trying experience. But they kept coming back. And by the last day of writing, most reported that the writing experience had been profoundly important for them.

The real test, however, was what would happen to these people in the weeks and months after the four days of expressive writing. With their permission, we were able to compare their physician visits due to illness before and after the study. Across our first four writing studies, those in the expressive writing condition made forty-three percent fewer doctor visits for illness than those who were asked to write about superficial topics. Most of the visits for both groups were for colds, flu, or other upper respiratory infections. Nevertheless, writing about personal traumas resulted in people seeing doctors at half their normal rate (Pennebaker & Beall 1986).

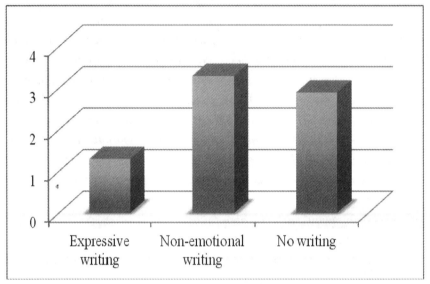

Figure 2. Yearly number of physician visits for illness in the three months after the experiment for participants in the emotional writing and control (non-emotional writing) conditions. The No Writing data is based on students who did not participate in the experiment.

If you are uncritical and like graphs, you might get very excited about the results depicted in Figure 2. But it's important to put these effects into perspective. These are statistical findings based on four studies with relatively healthy college students. They don't tell us who specifically may have benefited and who did not. They say nothing about why, when, and under what conditions writing might work. Most important, these results are not very helpful in answering the question, "Would writing help me deal with my life?"

What Are the Effects of Writing?

Since the first expressive writing studies were published in the 1980s, at least 300 studies about the benefits of expressive writing have been published. While the first studies focused almost exclusively on physician visits for illness, the scope of benefit measures has grown exponentially. As the number of studies increased, it became clear that writing was far more powerful than anyone ever dreamed.

Nearly thirty years later, we further appreciate the potential impact of expressive writing. We are now able to identify more clearly the areas where expressive writing is effective (Frattaroli 2006; Smyth & Pennebaker 2008).

Biological effects

We know that people go to the doctor less often after writing. So are there biological changes as a result of writing? Yes, and the effects generalize across several physiological systems. Recent reviews of expressive writing research suggest that expressive writing is a major medical advance (Stockdale 2011). Here are some of the ways expressive writing benefits those who write.

The immune system. The body's immune system can function more or less effectively, depending on the person's stress level. Labs at Ohio State, University of Miami, Auckland Medical School in New Zealand, and elsewhere find that emotional writing is associated with general enhancement in immune function (Koschwanez et al., 2013; Pennebaker, Kiecolt-Glasser & Glasser 1988; Lumley et al. 2011). Warning: We really don't know what these effects mean in terms of long-term health. However, we do understand that as expressive writing enhances emotion regulation, it can play a key role in brain and immune physiology (Petrie et al. 2004).

Medical markers of health. For their patients with chronic health problems, physicians often pay attention to specific indicators to determine whether the disease is being kept in check or getting worse. In recent years, researchers have found that for people who must manage chronic illnesses, expressive writing is associated with benefits. Asthma patients and rheumatoid arthritis patients showed improvements in lung function and joint mobility (Smyth & Arigo 2009; Smyth, Stone & Hurewitz, et al. 1999). Higher white blood cell counts were demonstrated among AIDS patients (Petrie et al. 2004). Patients with irritable bowel syndrome achieved a significant improvement in disease severity (Halpert, Rybin, & Doros 2010). Many studies of cancer patients demonstrate significant benefits in physical health, reduction in physical symptoms, a reduction in pain overall, better sleep, and higher daytime functioning (Henry et al. 2010; Low et al. 2010; De Moor et al. 2002; Rosenberg et al. 2002). Other studies with relatively healthy adults have found modest reductions in resting blood pressure levels (McGuire 2005) and lower liver enzyme levels often associated with excessive drinking (Francis & Pennebaker 1992). Arthritis and lupus patients who did expressive writing and who were specifically asked to describe the positive sides to their disease reported reduced fatigue that was maintained three months after writing (Danoff-Burg et al. 2006).

Physiological indicators of stress. Somewhat surprisingly, while people write or talk about traumas, they often show immediate signs of reduced stress: lower muscle tension in their face, and drops in hand skin conductance (often used in lie detection to measure the stress of deception and also easily measured with readily available Biodot® skin thermometers). Immediately after writing about emotional topics, people have lower blood pressure and heart rates (Pennebaker, Hughes, & O'Heeron 1987). Other researchers evaluated indicators of stress such as systolic and diastolic blood pressure, heart rate variability, and skin conductance. They found that expressive writing demonstrated benefits that lasted as long as four months (McGuire, Greenberg, & Gevirtz 2005).

Psychological Effects

The psychological and emotional effects of writing are a bit more complicated than we originally thought. We found it's instructive to distinguish between the immediate and long-term effects of expressive writing.

Mood changes immediately after writing: Feeling sad is normal. Immediately after writing about traumatic topics, people often feel worse — sad, even weepy. These effects are generally short-term and last an hour or two. Emotional writing can be likened to seeing a sad movie — afterwards you feel sadder but wiser. Being aware of this effect is extremely important. If you plan to write about important events in your life, give yourself time after writing to reflect.

Long-term mood changes. Writing may make you sad for a brief time after writing, but the long-term effects are far more positive. Across multiple studies, people who engage in expressive writing report feeling happier and less negative than they felt before writing. Similarly, reports of depressive symptoms, rumination, and general anxiety tend to drop in the weeks and months after writing about emotional upheavals (Lepore 1997). Other studies found improvement in overall well-being and improved cognitive functioning (Barclay & Skarlicki 2009).

Behavioral Changes

Writing does much more than affect your physical and mental health. You may actually start behaving differently.

Performance at school or work. Among beginning college students, expressive writing helps people adjust to their situation better. Consequently, at least three studies have found that students make higher grades in the semester after a writing study (Lumley & Provenzano 2003; Cameron & Nicholls 1998; Pennebaker, Colder, & Sharp 1990). This may be because emotional writing boosts people's working memory.

Working memory is the technical term for our general ability to think about complex tasks. If we are worrying about things — including emotional upheavals from the past — we have less working memory. Expressive writing, we now know, frees working memory, allowing us to deal with more complicated issues in our lives (Klein & Boals 2001). Students who did expressive writing about upcoming exams reported improved mood prior to their exams and improved performance (Dalton & Glenwick 2009; Frattaroli, Thomas, & Lyubomirsky 2011).

Some researchers believe that the benefits of expressive writing may be the result of increased exposure to the trauma, sometimes referred to as habituation. As people write about it time after time, their reactions to the experience become smaller and smaller. Other researchers explain that the benefits of expressive writing come from identifying, labeling, and integrating negative emotions into the broader context of one's life (Baddeley & Pennebaker 2011; De Giacomo et al. 2010; Sloan & Marx 2009).

Dealing with our social lives. Working with other people can sometimes be a daunting psychological task. The more emotional stress we are under, the more draining it is. Recent studies have suggested that expressive writing can enhance the quality of our social lives. In an attempt to explore this facet of writing, people were asked to wear a small tape recorder in the days before and after writing so that the researchers could monitor their social lives. Overall, people who wrote about traumatic experiences talked more with other people, laughed more easily and often, and used more positive emotion words in the weeks afterwards. Writing seemed to make people more socially comfortable — better listeners, talkers, indeed better friends and partners (Pennebaker & Graybeal 2001, Baddeley & Pennebaker 2011).

Studies demonstrate that expressive writing helps couples reduce anger, depression, and PTSD symptoms while couples are in psychotherapy after extramarital affairs (Snyder et al. 2004). Soldiers who did expressive writing about being reunited with their spouses and families after deployment improved their marital satisfaction (Baddeley & Pennebaker 2011).

Expressive writing may also be a method to alleviate anger and to make people better candidates for jobs. A few years ago, I collaborated on a project with middle-aged men who had unexpectedly been laid off from their high-tech jobs after working with the same company for over fifteen years. As a group, this was the most angry, hostile, unpleasant bunch I've ever worked with. Some of the participants were asked to write about their deepest emotions and thoughts about losing their jobs; the remainder wrote about how they used their time (part of America's peculiar obsession with time management). Eight months after writing, fifty-two percent of the emotional writing group had new jobs compared with only twenty percent of the time management participants. The two groups went on the same number of interviews. The only difference was that the expressive writers were offered jobs (Spera, Buhrfeind, & Pennebaker 1994).

In many ways, the layoff study speaks to the heart of this book. Here was a group of successful men whose lives unexpectedly fell apart on a cold January day. The job market was terrible, most men had to support a family, and at the same time they had to deal with the humiliation of losing their jobs. Most couldn't talk about their experience in any detail with their family, neighbors, or friends. Prior to the study, the few who had gone on job interviews were so full of hostility that their interviewers wanted nothing to do with them.

Only those men who were asked to address their emotions in writing benefited from the exercise. The writing helped them get past the experience. When they eventually went on job interviews in the months after writing, they were undoubtedly more at ease. They weren't compelled to tell their prospective employers how they had been abused by their last company. Writing helped transform these men from hostile ruminators into more open and accepting adults.

Who Benefits from Writing? Who Doesn't?

In any given study, some — but not all — people benefit from writing. Although a great deal of effort has been devoted to creating a profile of the writer who benefits, the research has met with only limited success. Here is what we know so far.

The writer's personality: sex, hostility, emotional awareness

All types of people seem to benefit from writing. Any personality differences that have been found have been remarkably subtle. One barely detectable difference, however, is the gender of the writer. Across a large number of studies, males tend to benefit more from writing than do females. In addition, people who tend to be naturally hostile and aggressive as well as out of touch with their own emotions show more health improvements after writing compared with their more easygoing, self-reflective, and open counterparts (Smyth 1998; Christensen, Edwards, Wiebe, et al. 1996).

Recent research finds that coping by repressing the memories or emotions of a trauma and the inability to find language or expression for emotions are linked to certain chronic conditions; these factors limit the ability of the immune system to function at its optimum. Studies show that maladaptive responses to stress increase an individual's overall risk for stress-related disorders and disease (Cusinato & L'Abate 2012; Stockdale 2011).

Hostile, out-of-touch males may be particularly good candidates for writing because they are the least likely to open up and talk with others. The more you can be yourself with your friends, the more likely you are to work through emotional upheavals. Keep in mind, however, that even the most emotionally expressive and open person in the world can sometimes get in a situation where he or she can't talk about a trauma or upheaval. In that case, writing can likely help.

Education or writing ability

Expressive writing studies have been conducted with people of widely varying educational levels and/or writing abilities. In some studies, the participants had no conception of spelling or grammar. It made no difference. They could still tell compelling and powerful stories. In other cases, I have worked with people who were so severely beaten down in their education that they were almost afraid to put anything into words for fear that I would slap them on their knuckles with a ruler.

Once they appreciated that their writing would not be graded, judged, or linked to them, their anxiety disappeared.

Recency and type of trauma

How recently a trauma occurred probably *is* important, however. Although there's been no systematic research on this, there is good reason to believe that writing is probably not beneficial if the trauma has occurred in the last few days. Depending on the severity of the trauma, people are often disoriented in the first one to three weeks after its occurrence. If you feel as though you are still reeling from a traumatic experience, then it is probably too early to start serious writing.

In terms of the type of trauma, we have not found any differences in the potential benefits of writing. Some researchers believe that the more unexpected and unwanted the upheaval, the more likely that expressive writing will yield positive effects. For example, a research group from Holland finds that writing about the natural death of a close friend or family member brings no clear benefits (Stroebe, Stroebe, Zech, et al. 2002). In a way, this makes sense. An expected death is part of the natural order of things. We are comfortable talking with others about the event, and our friends usually know how to act, what to say, and what to expect.

Culture, class, and language

Positive effects have been found for expressive writing in countries around the globe: United States, Japan, New Zealand, Mexico, Holland, Germany, Spain, England, Hungary, Poland, and Texas. Writing in any language appears to work — either the person's native or learned language. Similarly, people can be in upper, middle, or lower social classes in these countries, and writing continues to bring benefits (Lepore & Smyth 2002; Pennebaker 1997).

Do Certain Ways of Writing Work Better than Others?

One of the main debates in the writing world these days concerns how and why writing works. We have gradually been discovering that some ways of framing the writing technique are more effective than others are. Some of these variations are introduced in the writing exercises in Part II and Part III of this book.

Writing versus talking

Does talking about a trauma work as well as writing about it? It depends. One study compared talking into a tape recorder with writing. Both techniques were equally beneficial. Talking to a real person about a trauma is far more complex. If the other person can accept you no matter what you say and you can be completely honest in your disclosure, then talking may actually be better than writing. But therein is the rub. If the person you are confiding in does not react favorably to you and to what you say, then talking may actually be *worse* than not confiding at all.

What about writing and then reading to someone else what you have written? Same problem. If your audience doesn't react well to you, you may come away with even more negative feelings. The only study that has found negative effects of emotional writing required trauma patients to write about their traumas and then read their stories to other people in a group. Contrary to the researchers' expectations, this public reading of their traumas made the patients more depressed (Gidron, Peri, Connolly, et al. 1996).

Safety in writing: The role of an audience

People usually don't talk about emotional upheavals because they fear the reactions of others. The purpose of expressive writing is for you to be completely honest and open with yourself. Your audience is you and you alone. Studies have shown that when people disclose a trauma to someone they don't know or trust, they hold back — and don't show benefits.

Unlike every paper you wrote in high school, expressive writing doesn't need to be read by anyone in order for you to benefit from it. In a study in our lab several years ago, (Pennebaker 1997) we asked students to write about a trauma either on regular paper or on a child's magic pad. (Remember magic pads? You write on a gray plastic sheet and when you lift the sheet, all the writing disappears). The same benefits accrued. Actually, recent research suggests that writing at a distance from a professional helper has solid potential benefit. Studies in distance writing suggest that the Internet may facilitate this quite well (Baddeley & Pennebaker 2011; L'Abate & Sweeney 2011).

Writing Style

Some ways of writing appear to work better than others do. Recent studies by multiple labs are converging on some common guidelines. People tend to benefit most from expressive writing if they:

Openly acknowledge emotions. Emotional experience is part of a trauma. The ability to feel and label both the negative *and* the positive feelings that occurred during and following the trauma is important.

Work to construct a coherent story. Immediately after a trauma, things often seem out of control and disconnected. One goal of expressive writing is to begin to put things together again. One way of accomplishing this is to make a meaningful story of what happened and how it is affecting you. Many argue that the brain is a narrative organ and that story-making is hardwired into our very nature. Creating a narrative, including a coherent beginning, middle, and end, is a well-documented part of trauma treatment and holds much promise for benefits from writing about trauma.

Switch perspectives. People who have experienced a trauma initially see it from one perspective — their own. Indeed, when individuals first write about a massive upheaval, they first describe what they saw, felt, and experienced. Recent studies indicate that people who benefit the most from writing have been able to see events through others' eyes. Indeed, even writing about a personal event in the third person has proven beneficial (Andersson & Conley 2013; Campbell & Pennebaker 2003; Seih et al. 2011).

Find your voice. A guiding principle of expressive writing is that you express yourself openly and honestly. People who write in a cold, detached manner and who quote Shakespeare, Aristotle, or Henry Ford may be fine historians and may even write a great editorial in the local newspaper. But impressive writing is not the point of expressive writing. People who benefit the most from writing are able to find a voice that reflects who they are.

Writing by Hand or Typing

Many people intuitively think that writing longhand is more beneficial than typing. Indeed, it is slower and allows them more time to think about what they are writing. However, the few studies that have examined the ways of writing have not found any significant differences (Brewin & Lennard 1999). Most researchers would probably recommend that you write using whatever mode you find most comfortable.

Some Potential Dangers of Writing

The way that expressive writing has been portrayed up to now makes it sound like the world's greatest cure-all. Start writing today and you will get a new job, your health will improve, and you will be loved and admired by everyone. It sounds almost too good to be true. It is. There are both imagined and real dangers to expressive writing that are often not appreciated.

A very minor concern: Losing control

In some quarters, there is a belief that some people are barely holding on to their sanity. Even mentioning something upsetting can cause these people to go insane — to flip out in a most unseemly manner. An extension of this thinking is that if people are asked to write about emotional upheavals, a certain proportion will start uncontrollably screaming, ranting, and frothing at the mouth.

I suppose it could happen. However, in the thousands of people I have seen write, it hasn't happened yet. On a few occasions, people have cried and become quite sad. On three occasions in twenty years, we have taken people to a psychologist. But all three wanted back in the study the next day.

As will be discussed in greater detail in the next chapter, we have instituted the *Flip-Out Rule* in our research and workshops. It's very simple: If you feel you will get too upset when you write about a particular topic, don't write about it. If you think that something you will say will cause you to flip out, don't say it. This rule is very simple and has been quite effective.

A minimal concern: Overanalyzing and navel-gazing

Self-reflective writing should be viewed as a course-correction mechanism. If you are dealing with a traumatic experience, it is important to analyze it, try to understand it, and to get on with life. Occasionally, people will begin to reflect on an emotional upheaval and become completely obsessed with it. Their four-day writing procedure expands to forty days and then four thousand days. They often begin telling the same stories over and over, never finding any resolution.

There is convincing evidence that writing about the same topic in the same way day after day is not at all helpful — and may possibly be harmful. You can analyze something too much. If, after several days of writing, you feel that you are not making any progress, then you need to rethink your writing strategy. Try some other approaches in this book. If those don't seem to be working, consider talking to a professional — a therapist, social worker, minister, or a trustworthy friend.

A moderate concern: Blackmail and humiliation

In the child abuse literature, one of the most troubling stories concerns instances where children tell their mothers or fathers about sexual abuse and their parents either don't believe them or blame them for causing it. The evidence suggests that in many cases, these children would have been better off keeping the abuse secret.

What if you write about your deepest emotions and thoughts and someone reads your journal? Over the years, I have heard of many instances where a spouse, parent, or friend read a person's diary and it changed their relationship forever — often in a bad way. Your writing must be private and for you alone. If someone might read your expressive writing, then hide or destroy it. Be careful that what you write on electronic devices isn't automatically shared. It is bad enough dealing with major emotional upheavals in your life. You don't need someone judging you.

A serious concern: Potential life changes

We live our lives in a web of connections. Changing one thing in our lives has the potential to affect many others around us. The ways you are dealing with a trauma may actually be exactly what your friends and family desire most. If you change your coping strategies, you might affect your closest relationships in ways you never imagined. Two stories illustrate this problem.

First, several years ago, I worked with a young woman whose husband had suddenly died almost a year earlier. Through her coworkers, I learned that she was viewed as a pillar of strength — she had been happy, courageous, even inspirational in her optimism in the wake of her loss. She came to me because she felt she needed to write about the death, which she did. By the last day of writing, she was transformed. She was more relaxed, her blood pressure was lower, and she was deeply appreciative about the writing experience.

Two months later, we met to discuss her life and the writing intervention. In the interim, she had quit her job, stopped seeing her friends at work, and had moved back to her hometown. All changes she'd made, she said, as a result of the writing. Because of the writing experience, she realized that she was on a life path she didn't want. She was putting on a false cheerful front for her current friends, and she discovered that the only people she could be truly honest with were her childhood friends.

Was writing good for her? Some would say that it undermined her career, her financial future, and her entire social network. She, however, maintained it was a life-saver.

A second case is even more striking. A woman in her early forties with three children told me of her need to write in order to deal with a series of terrible childhood events that still haunted her. After several days of writing, she reported that she felt free for the first time in her life. Over the next few months, she left her husband, and with her children moved into low-income housing, where she barely eked out a living. She went through a period of deep, almost suicidal depression from which she gradually escaped.

In a recent interview, she maintained that the writing was the direct cause of her divorce, depression, and poverty. But she, like the woman whose husband died, is still grateful for the writing. Deep down, she claims, she knew she had to address basic issues in her life that had been causing her profound conflict and unhappiness. The cost was higher than she'd anticipated, but in retrospect, it was worth it.

These two cases suggest that writing can be a significant threat. By reducing your inner conflicts, you may affect the course of your life and the lives of others in unintended ways. Statistics have shown that most people report that the life changes following writing have been beneficial. Indeed, even these two individuals are appreciative of the power of expressive writing.

Nothing is as simple as it seems.

Expressive writing is a self-reflective tool with tremendous power. By exploring emotional upheavals in our lives, we are forced to look inward and examine who we are. This occasional self-examination can serve as a life-course correction. In the pages that follow, think about the various aspects of expressive writing and how it can benefit you.

2

How Can We Get Ready To Write?

In the next chapter, we outline a basic writing exercise. A four-day writing approach has been found to be effective in improving people's mental and physical health. What the simple writing instructions don't convey is the power of the writing context. We have learned that *how*, *when,* and *where* you write can sometimes be as important as *what* you write.

This chapter will help you set the stage for your writing. Indeed, think of writing as a form of ritual. For it to have maximal effect, it's best to write in a meaningful place, time, and atmosphere. As you set up the context for your writing, let's begin with what your writing topic should be.

What Should You Write?

On its surface, this book describes dealing with emotional upheavals or traumas. What is perplexing about traumas, however, is that they directly or indirectly influence every part of your life. Which means you might start writing about a clear, unambiguous traumatic experience but then find yourself writing about something else. For example, I have seen many cases where a person starts writing about the death of a parent as their traumatic experience and, within fifteen minutes, they devote most of their energy to writing about marriage issues. That's okay.

Here are some simple guidelines.

Write about what keeps you awake at night. The emotional upheaval bothering you the most and keeping you awake at night is a good place to start writing. In most cases, this is quite straightforward. You know why you are having sleep problems, why you keep thinking of the upheaval. Begin with this upheaval, but if you find yourself moving to another topic, go with it.

Write to learn where you need to go. Trust where your writing takes you. You may start with a trauma but soon begin writing about other topics. As long as these other topics are emotionally important, follow them. If, however, you find yourself writing about what you would like for dinner — or some other distracting topic — then force yourself back to the trauma. Also, if you find yourself getting bored with your trauma writing, switch topics. Look for another emotional topic that keeps you awake at night or occupies your thoughts during the day. Also consider any topic you have been actively avoiding.

Write about issues relevant to the here and now. We have all dealt with painful experiences in our lives that we no longer think about and that don't appear to affect us in the present. If dredging up these old issues isn't relevant to your life right now, why write about them? Let sleeping dogs lie.

Write only about traumas that are present in your mind. A remarkable amount of literature deals with repressed memories. The repressed memory literature explores the idea that people have had horrible childhood experiences that they don't remember — many of which involved childhood sexual abuse. The writing you are doing here focuses on what you are aware of now. If you have no memory of a given childhood experience, why not go with the working assumption that it never happened? After all, you wouldn't know the difference anyway. Write only about conscious traumas and upheavals. It will save you thousands of dollars in therapy and legal bills.

How Much Time Should You Write?

Virtually every study conducted with expressive writing has asked people to write for about twenty minutes on three or four consecutive days. For the purpose of this book, that's all that I'm requesting as well. Promise yourself that you will try expressive writing for four days. That's all. If you want to write more, do it. If you want to try other writing exercises suggested in the later chapters in the book, great. If you want to try a more extended approach, follow the six-week program described in Part III of this book. But to see if expressive writing can be helpful for you, use Chapter 3 as a guide and arrange to write for twenty minutes each day for four days.

How frequently to write. While there is some debate about whether it is better to write for four consecutive days or to separate your writing days, there is nothing conclusive either way. One study, for example, reported that it might be better to write once a week for four consecutive weeks. Your schedule and the urgency you feel in dealing with any emotional upheavals you are living with play a role in what will work for you. My personal experience is that writing for four consecutive days is a bit more efficient. Let your own schedule be your guide, but why not try the most common existing model first and then see what else might work for you.

How long for each session. In most large-scale studies, people wrote for around twenty minutes on three to four occasions. Recent research, however, suggests that people can benefit from writing if they write for briefer amounts of time — as few as five minutes on each occasion.

Although there is no official recommendation, most experts would probably urge someone just beginning expressive writing to set aside twenty minutes for the first few times.

What if you want to keep writing after twenty minutes? Then keep writing. The twenty-minute rule is an arbitrary minimum. That is, plan to write for at least twenty minutes each day with the understanding that you can write more, but you shouldn't write less.

How many days to write. What if you find that you enjoy writing and want to continue past four days? Do it. Many people find that once they begin writing, they realize they have many issues to think about. Write for as many days as you need — just think of the four days as a minimum.

Booster-writing sessions. Think of expressive writing as a tool always be at your disposal, or like having medicine in your medicine cabinet. No need to take the medicine when you are healthy, but when you are under the weather, you can always turn to it. Once you have tried writing as a healing agent, try it again when you need to. Also, you might find that in the future, you won't need to write for four days, twenty minutes a day. Merely writing occasionally when something bothers you might be sufficient.

Writing prescription: To Journal or Not to Journal?

Sometimes a healthcare provider may tell a patient, "You should write about that in a journal," but that's as far as the prescription goes. You may wonder, is keeping a daily journal a good idea? Ironically, there is no clear evidence that keeping a daily journal or diary is good for your health, perhaps in part because once people get in the habit of writing every day, they devote less and less time to dealing with important psychological issues. Sometimes a journal can become a worn path with little benefit. Writing in a journal about the same trauma, using the same words, expressing the same feelings over and over is a bit like the grandmother in Eudora Welty's story, *A Worn Path*. The woman in this story travels the same path every year at the same time, seeking medicine for a child who died years before. No medicine will bring back the grandmother's dead child. Writing in a journal every day about that same issue with the same words in the same way will probably not bring the relief you seek and may actually do more harm than good.

My own experience is that journal writing works best on an as-needed basis as a life-course correction. If your life is going well, you are happy, and are not obsessing about things in the past, why overanalyze yourself? Let it go and enjoy life as it comes. It is safe to say that some future miseries will visit you again. When they happen, do some expressive writing to deal with them.

When Should You Write?

Without getting too philosophical here, it is true that multiple issues of *time* must be addressed — from time of life to time of day. For instance, what about time after a trauma?

How soon after a Trauma?

Traumas and emotional upheavals can be tricky. Some happen quickly and end abruptly. Others never seem to end. In deciding to write, consider the following issues:

Recent trauma. If you have faced a massive traumatic experience in your life within the last two to three weeks, it may be too early for you to write about it. At the very least, it may be too soon for you to deal with some of the deeper emotions that the trauma has awakened. If the trauma or emotional upheaval is too raw, begin your writing in a relatively safe way, perhaps describing what is happening in your life right now. As you feel comfortable, you can begin dealing with the trauma and its effects more deeply. If you don't feel ready to write, then don't. Come back to this book in a few weeks.

Present trauma. Writing about an ongoing emotional upheaval is a good way to manage feelings and achieve relief. Some traumas and emotional upheavals have a life of their own — they are always around in one form or another. Some examples include living with a fatal or chronic disease, going through a divorce, or dealing with an abusive parent or spouse. The list is endless. For situations like this, writing has been found to be beneficial. You might find that writing for four days now makes a big difference. However, as your emotional event unfolds in the future, additional writing may be helpful as well.

Past trauma. The original writing technique was designed for people who had experienced a traumatic experience in the past — a month or even decades ago. Writing is particularly recommended if you find yourself thinking, worrying, or dreaming about the event too much. It can also help if you find that this upheaval is adversely affecting your present life in some way.

Future trauma. Is it helpful to write about the eventual death of a loved one? Or a divorce that you know is coming? Or something else in the future? Sure, why not? It's free. But in your writing, explore why you are having the feelings and how these feelings relate to other issues in your life. Remember that the point of this writing is how we make sense of a troubling experience or event and how we incorporate that experience into the entire story of our lives.

Is This a Good Time in Your Life to Write?

Expressive writing can force you to deal with important emotional experiences that you may have been avoiding. Oftentimes, people think and talk with others about these events in some detail over the course of writing. Some times in your life may be better than others for dealing with emotional upheavals. All things being equal, the following times would be preferable if you have the luxury of choosing your writing time:

- You are on vacation.
- It's the beginning of a weekend.
- You are not inundated with other tasks.
- You have some time to yourself after each day's writing to self-reflect.

Unfortunately, emotional upheavals often come along at inconvenient times. Upheavals also have the nasty habit of *creating* inconveniences. Consequently, you may have to write at a time that is hectic and out of control. That's far better than not writing at all.

What's the Best Time of Day to Write?

I'm a big believer in trying to write at the same time every day if at all possible. Part of this is to establish a writing ritual. As much as possible, it is critical to consider what you will be doing after each day's writing. At least two studies have suggested that people need some reflection time after their writing (Smyth & Pennebaker 2008; Petrie, Booth, & Pennebaker 1998). That is, you don't want to set up your writing so that as soon as you finish, you go straight into an important business meeting.

In the very popular book *The Artist's Way*, Julia Cameron (2002) suggests that people can greatly benefit from relatively unstructured writing exercises every morning as soon as they wake up. In her mind, this is a way to clear the mind before beginning the day. Although I'm not familiar with any research to support this idea, intuitively I think it makes good sense. Writing about traumatic experience in the morning may work as well; if you have some free time afterwards, then mornings might be a good time to write.

Across multiple studies, we have had the most success with people writing at the end of their workday. If you have children and need to feed them, then after they have gone to bed might be a good time. The operative rule, however, is for you to have some free time after writing to let your mind reflect on what you have written.

Where Should You Write?

Consider the construction of healing environments. Most physician offices and hospitals have common layouts, smells, lighting, and uniforms. Once you enter these situations, you get a subtle sense of cleanliness, science, order, structure, and yes, physical healing. Churches, temples, and mosques all have their own unique environments as well. As you enter them, you can often feel your body relax and change.

Think of the expressive writing method as your own healing ritual. Because you are your own physician or priest or goddess, you get to create your own setting. Based on my own research with writing, certain suggestions come to mind:

Creating a unique environment. It's ideal to have a place for your writing where you typically *don't* work. If your living arrangement is such that you can't get any privacy, go to a library, religious establishment, a coffee shop, or even a park. Wherever you go to write should afford a sense of comfort and security.

Most people prefer to write at home. If you have a special room where you can write, make the space a little different than usual. Change the lighting, for example. In one series of studies, we covered lamps with red cellophane and put them on the floor to create odd shadows. We wanted to make the room look like no other. Wherever you choose to write, create your own space, both figuratively and literally, where you are comfortable writing.

Creating a ritual for writing. As part of establishing a unique environment, think about setting it up in the same way each day. You might consider lighting a candle and ceremonially putting it out when you are finished writing. Some people have used incense to make a distinctive smell. Others have brought pictures or objects into their writing area as a way to symbolically bring in the emotional event.

Your ritual may begin before writing and extend to the time after writing. It is not uncommon for people to exercise or engage in meditation before or after writing each day. A long shower or bath before or after writing can also be a cleansing ritual. Similarly, putting on a cap, a particular blouse or shirt, or wearing nothing at all can be a signal for you to get into your writing. You are the boss. Create the environment and ritual best suited to your personality.

What Technology Do You Need to Write?

Some people prefer to buy their own journal book, and others would rather write directly on a computer. Whether you write in a book, on paper, or a computer makes no difference in terms of the value of writing. The value comes in the actual writing.

Many people want explicit instructions about the details of writing. Should you use a pen or pencil? Does color matter? It's up to you. Do you prefer writing with a pen? Then use a pen. Do you prefer a blue pencil? Ditto. Invisible ink? It's up to you.

And Finally, The Flip-Out Rule

I hereby declare you ready to begin your expressive writing experience. But before you start, it is important to review ***The Flip-Out Rule***.

> *If you feel that writing about a particular topic is too much for you to handle, then do not write about it. If you know that you aren't ready to address a particularly painful topic, then write about something else. When you are ready, then tackle the other topic. If you feel that you will flip out by writing, don't write.*

What could be simpler?
Enjoy your writing.

3

What Are the Basic Writing Techniques?

This chapter presents the essential features of the expressive writing method. The instructions have been drawn from dozens of successful writing studies. For this exercise, your goal is to write of a minimum of twenty minutes per day for four consecutive days. It is okay to skip days, but the sooner you complete the four-day exercise, the better.

In addition to following the writing instructions, complete the brief questionnaire at the end of each day's writing. The questionnaire is a rough indicator of how the writing is affecting you. Once you have finished all four days of writing, go back and evaluate how your impressions have evolved over time. The next chapter, Chapter 4, will walk you through ways of analyzing and thinking about your writing.

General Instructions

For the next four days, you will write about a trauma or emotional upheaval that has profoundly affected your life. A few simple guidelines to keep in mind while you are writing:

Write for twenty minutes a day. If you end up writing for more than twenty minutes, that's great. However, the following day, you still need to write for at least twenty minutes.

Writing topic. You can write about the same event on all four days or about different events each day. Not everyone has had a major trauma they want to write about. However, all of us have had major conflicts or stressors in our lives — you can write about those as well. What you choose to write about should be something that is extremely personal and important for you.

Write continuously. Once you begin writing, write without stopping. Don't worry about spelling or grammar. Your high school English teacher will never see it. If you run out of things to say, simply repeat what you have already written.

Write only for yourself. You are writing for yourself and no one else. Plan on destroying or hiding what you have written when you are finished. Do not make this a letter to someone. If, after you finish writing, you want to write a letter, then do it. But this exercise is for your eyes only.

The Flip-Out Rule. If you feel as though you cannot write about a particular event because it will push you over the edge, then don't write about it. Deal only with those events or situations that you can handle now. If you have additional traumatic topics that you can't get to now, you can deal with them in the future.

What to expect after writing. Many people often feel somewhat sad or depressed after writing, especially on the first day or two. If this happens to you, it is completely normal. These feelings usually last only a few minutes and, in some cases, hours — much like the way you feel after seeing a sad movie. If possible, plan to have some time to yourself after writing to reflect on the issues you have been dealing with.

Day One Writing Instructions

Remember that this is the first of four days of writing. In today's writing, your goal is to write about your deepest thoughts and feelings about the trauma or emotional upheaval that has been influencing your life the most. In your writing, really let go and explore this event and how it has affected you. Today, it may be beneficial to simply write about the event itself, how you felt when it was occurring, and how you feel now.

As you write about this upheaval, you might begin to tie it to other parts of your life. For example, how is it related to your childhood and your relationships with your parents and close family? How is the event connected to those people you have most loved, feared, or been angry with? How is this upheaval related to your current life — your friends and family, your work, and your place in life? And above all, how is this event related to who you have been in the past, who you would like to be in the future, and who you are now?

In today's writing, it is particularly important that you really let go and examine your deepest emotions and thoughts surrounding this upheaval in your life. Remember to write continuously the entire twenty minutes. And never forget that this writing is for you and you alone.

At the conclusion of your twenty minutes of writing, read the section "Post-writing thoughts" and complete the post-writing questionnaire.

Post-Writing Thoughts Following the Day One Writing Session

Congratulations! You have completed the first day of writing. After each writing exercise, it can be helpful to make objective assessments about how the writing felt. In this way, you can go back and determine which writing methods are most effective for you.

For this and for all future writing exercises, respond to each of the five following questions either at the end of your writing or in a separate place. Put a number between 0 and 10 by each question.

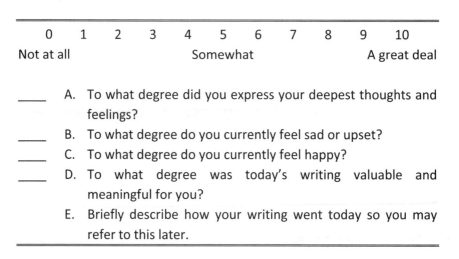

	0	1	2	3	4	5	6	7	8	9	10
Not at all					Somewhat						A great deal

_____ A. To what degree did you express your deepest thoughts and feelings?

_____ B. To what degree do you currently feel sad or upset?

_____ C. To what degree do you currently feel happy?

_____ D. To what degree was today's writing valuable and meaningful for you?

E. Briefly describe how your writing went today so you may refer to this later.

For many people, the first day of writing is the most difficult. This kind of writing can bring up emotions and thoughts that you may not have known that you had. It may also have flowed much more easily than you expected — especially if you wrote about something that you have been keeping to yourself for a long time.

If you don't want anyone to see your writing, keep the pages in a secure place or destroy them. If keeping them is not a problem, you can go back and analyze the pages at the end of the four days of writing.

Now, take some time for yourself. Until tomorrow.

Day Two Writing Instructions

Today is the second day of the four-day process. In your last writing session, you were asked to explore your thoughts and feelings about a trauma or emotional upheaval that has affected you deeply. In today's writing, your task is to *really* examine your very deepest emotions and thoughts. You can write about the same trauma or upheaval as you did yesterday or a completely different one.

The writing instructions today are similar to those of your last writing session. Today, try to link the trauma to other parts of your life. Remember that a trauma or emotional upheaval can often influence every aspect of your life — your relationships with friends and family, how you and others view you, your work, and even how you think about your past. In today's writing, begin thinking how this upheaval is affecting your life in general. You might also write about how you may be responsible for some of the effects of the trauma.

As before, write continuously for the entire twenty minutes and open up your deepest thoughts and feelings. At the conclusion of your writing, complete the post-writing questionnaire.

Thoughts Following the Day Two Writing Session

You have completed the second of the four-day writing exercise. Before setting aside your writing for the day, please complete the following questionnaire. Put a number between 0 and 10 by each question.

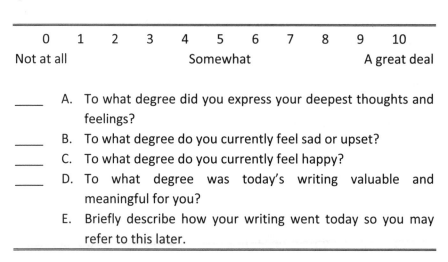

0	1	2	3	4	5	6	7	8	9	10
Not at all					Somewhat					A great deal

_____ A. To what degree did you express your deepest thoughts and feelings?

_____ B. To what degree do you currently feel sad or upset?

_____ C. To what degree do you currently feel happy?

_____ D. To what degree was today's writing valuable and meaningful for you?

       E. Briefly describe how your writing went today so you may refer to this later.

You now have two days of writing to compare. Look at the numbers on the questionnaire from the first day and from today's writing. How did today compare with your first day? Did you notice that your topic was shifting? How about the way you were writing? Between now and your next writing, think about what you have written. Are you starting to see things in a different light? How is writing affecting your emotions?

Now give yourself a little time to step back from your writing. Until tomorrow.

Day Three Writing Instructions

You have made it through two days of writing. After today, you will have only one more day of writing. Tomorrow, then, you need to wrap up your story. Today, however, continue to explore your deepest thoughts and emotions about the topics you have been tackling so far.

On the surface, today's writing assignment is very similar to the earlier assignments. In your writing, you can focus on the same topics you have been examining or you can shift your focus to either another trauma or to some other feature of the same trauma. Your primary goal, however, is to focus on your emotions and thoughts about those events that are affecting your life the most right now.

It is important that you don't repeat what you have already written in your past exercises. Writing about the same general topic is fine, but you also need to explore it from different perspectives and in different ways. As you write about this emotional upheaval, what are you feeling and thinking? How has this event shaped your life and who you are?

In today's writing, allow yourself to explore those deep issues about which you may be particularly vulnerable. As always, write continuously the entire twenty minutes.

Thoughts Following the Day-Three Writing Session

You have completed the next-to-last day of writing. Please complete the following questionnaire using a number between 0 and 10 by each question.

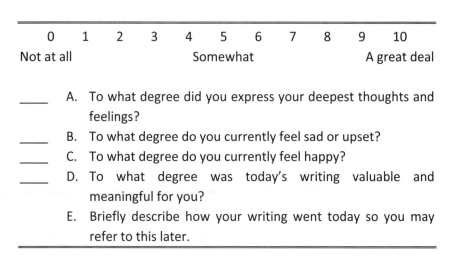

0	1	2	3	4	5	6	7	8	9	10
Not at all					Somewhat					A great deal

____ A. To what degree did you express your deepest thoughts and feelings?

____ B. To what degree do you currently feel sad or upset?

____ C. To what degree do you currently feel happy?

____ D. To what degree was today's writing valuable and meaningful for you?

E. Briefly describe how your writing went today so you may refer to this later.

In most studies, the third day of writing is highly significant. People often arrive at critical issues they have been avoiding. Whereas the first two writing sessions can be like putting toes in the water to see if it's too cold, by the third day some people are ready to jump completely in. A second group of people open up most on the first day. By the third day of writing, this second group sometimes is beginning to run out of steam. Both patterns are associated with improved health.

As with your last writing exercise, try to compare what you have written across the three sessions. What issues are surfacing as most important for you? Have you been surprised by any of your feelings while you were writing? Has the writing provoked any thoughts during the periods that you have been away from it?

Remember that tomorrow is the final day of the four-day writing exercise. The instructions for your last assignment will be much like today's. Since it will be the final day, however, think about how you will tie things up.

Now pamper yourself a bit. Until tomorrow.

Day Four Writing Instructions

This is the final day of the four-day writing exercise. As with the previous days' writings, explore your deepest emotions and thoughts about those upheavals and issues in your life that are most important and troublesome for you. Stand back and think about the events, issues, thoughts, and feelings that you have disclosed. In your writing, try to tie up anything that you haven't yet confronted. What are your emotions and thoughts at this point? What things have you learned, lost, and gained as a result of this upheaval in your life? How will these past events guide your thoughts and actions in the future?

Really let go in your writing and be honest with yourself about this upheaval. Do your best to wrap up the entire experience into a meaningful story that you can take with you into the future.

Thoughts Following the Final Writing Session

You have completed the last day of writing. Please complete the following questionnaire using a number between 0 and 10 by each question.

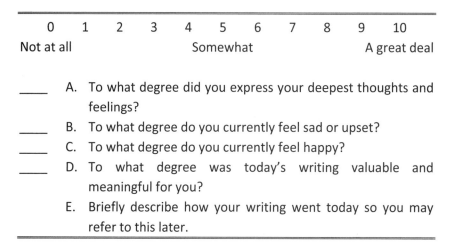

Today concludes the basic four-day writing exercise. Most people find the last day of writing the least enjoyable. This is often a sign that you are tired of dealing with this trauma and want to get on with other life tasks.

In some ways, it is tempting to go back over the various writing samples, questionnaire responses, and personal observations immediately after the fourth writing day. Indeed, it is important to review your writing. However, it is strongly recommended that you take at least two or three days off from the writing exercise before you do this. When you are ready to begin assessing your writing, turn to the next chapter.

4

How Can We Look Back at Our Writing?

Did the four-day writing exercise make a difference in your life? If so, it can be helpful to dissect what aspects may have been *most* helpful, so you can structure your own writing exercises in the future to maximize the potential of your writing. If you feel that you did not gain any benefits from expressive writing, do some serious troubleshooting to see what might have gone wrong.

To get maximum benefit from this chapter, read it several days or even weeks after you have completed the four-day writing exercise. However, if you have just finished the writing and want to know more, go ahead and read the chapter now, but come back to it after some time has elapsed. If you saved your writings, have them with you.

Measuring Change

Perhaps it's my scientific side, but I believe it is important to document any changes the writing may have brought about. Compare how you have been feeling and behaving in the last day or two with the days before you started writing. Have you noticed some of the following changes?

★ *Feeling more positive emotions; finding it easier to laugh*
★ *Taking less time to fall asleep; better sleep in general*
★ *Feeling healthier, fewer aches and pains*

★ *Drinking less alcohol, taking fewer drugs, eating more healthily*

★ *Thinking about the trauma less often, and when you do think about it, the thoughts are less painful*

★ *Feeling less irritable, having fewer disagreements or fights with others (the sense that other people seem nicer)*

★ *Experiencing more honest and open relationships with others*

★ *Finding it easier to focus on work and get things done*

★ *Noticing a greater sense of meaning in your life; a better understanding of the emotional upheaval you have written about*

These are some of the most common findings in the research literature on expressive writing. If you noticed changes in at least some of these feelings or behaviors, expressive writing is probably a good coping system for you. Indeed, you might find additional value in experimenting with other writing strategies that are outlined in this book.

What if the writing has made you feel worse rather than better? This can happen in a small percentage of cases and is a normal reaction. If you feel as though you are in particularly bad shape — feelings of deep depression, self-destructive thoughts, potentially dangerous behaviors — you need to talk to someone. Several phone numbers for crisis counseling are available in the Resources section at the end of the book.

If you didn't benefit from writing but still feel there's some potential in it for you, read the rest of this chapter. There may be some secrets that you can uncover in your writing that can guide you in the future.

Looking at the Writings

If you wrote longhand (rather than on a computer or in your e-reader) and saved your writing samples, stand back and look at them as if you were a scientist who didn't speak English. Start with your handwriting. Did the overall neatness of your writing change from day to day? How about the slant of your writing? Many people change their writing as they gradually deal with an upsetting experience.

Look at the handwriting of a woman who wrote for four days about a deeply upsetting sexual experience that happened to her when she was a young teenager. On the first day, she was very controlled in describing the event. But as she wrote more on the following days, her handwriting became more expressive. In many ways, the way she wrote mirrored the changes in her thinking about the event over time.

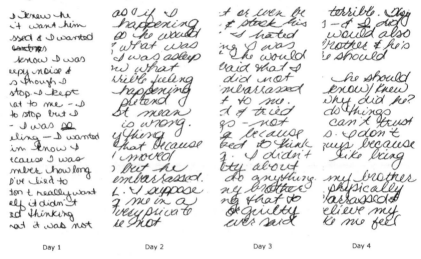

Day 1   Day 2   Day 3   Day 4

Figure 3. A handwriting sample from a woman writing about the same emotional upheaval across the four-day writing exercise

In addition, pay attention to strike-outs or erasures. When people are editing themselves — or controlling the way they appear — it is common for them to carefully edit their writing as they go along. Mark-outs and corrections also hint that the person is paying more attention to *how* they are writing than to *what* they are writing.

Finally, an almost infinite number of other ways to analyze writing exist for you. Look at changes in spelling, use of particular words, the pressure you were exerting on the paper as you were writing, or changes in punctuation or even page layout from day to day. How do these stylistic changes map onto the topics you were dealing with? Keep in mind that no one knows how these changes might reveal your psychological makeup. You, however, will be the best detective for this project.

Eyeing the Numbers

At the conclusion of each day's writing, you were given four brief questions about your writing. If you completed the questionnaire items, look back over them. The first question asked the degree to which you expressed your deepest emotions and thoughts that day. Using the 10-point scale, most people will mark an 8, 9, or 10 — indicating that they were quite expressive in their writing. The one exception that we sometimes find is on the last day. Many people are often psychologically finished with their writing on the last day and can't find the energy to delve into their thoughts and emotions to the same degree they had on previous days.

If you reported a number 5 or less across most of the writing days, what was going on for you? If you felt that writing was not particularly beneficial — and at the same time you didn't express your emotions and thoughts a great deal — this might explain why.

The next questions asked how sad and happy you were feeling after writing. Interestingly, most people feel relatively sad after writing — particularly on the first days. However, individuals generally become less sad each day. This drop in sadness and a corresponding increase in happiness indicate you're benefiting from the exercise. You might also explore how the topics you addressed were related to your mood changes. Did some topics affect you in ways you weren't expecting?

In many ways, the last questionnaire item was the most important one. You were asked to evaluate the degree to which each day's writing was valuable and meaningful for you. If your numbers were consistently low (5 or lower), then rethink how you were approaching the writing exercise. It may be that writing isn't a particularly helpful strategy for you. Alternatively, this type of writing may not be useful, but other types could be. Be sure and read the next section before deciding what to do.

Analyzing Your Writings

Are some ways of writing more beneficial than others? This question is mystifying the research world these days. In theory, if we can find certain ways of writing that are the most healthy, we can prescribe them to people. Notice how very little was said in the first part of the book about how to write? That's because the research community still hasn't figured out what works best.

But there are some promising findings on the horizon. In the last few years, researchers have been analyzing the writing samples of people who benefited from writing as well as from people who did not benefit. Although the results are based on fairly esoteric linguistic analyses, they may have value for you in interpreting your own writing.

Expressing emotions in writing

Traumatic experiences, by their very nature, elicit powerful and complex emotions. We have known for a long time that people who do not or cannot refer to their feelings when writing about a trauma tend not to benefit from the writing exercise.

Use negative emotions in moderation. More interesting, however, is the relative use of negative versus positive emotions in writing. Traumas, of course, tend to be associated with a host of negative emotions: sadness, guilt, anger, anxiety, and depression. Not being able to express or acknowledge these real feelings can be a problem. Sometimes people don't express these feelings because they were viewed as "unacceptable" emotions somewhere in their past. Having emotions is not a question of right or wrong — emotions just *are*. If you feel an emotion while writing about a trauma, admit it on paper.

The odd thing about negative emotions, however, is that they need to be acknowledged — but not dwelt upon. Across multiple studies, people who use the most negative emotion words (e.g., *hate, cry, hurt, afraid*) while writing about traumas tended not to benefit much from the writing experience. It may be those people are in a spiral of self-pity. Perhaps too much focus on their negative feelings may blind people to the broader meaning of an emotional upheaval. Finally, it could be that an excessive use of negative emotions in writing signals that the writer is deeply depressed. Indeed, people who are profoundly depressed may not benefit from writing until their depression lifts. (Note: if you are deeply depressed, seek help. See the Resources section for suggestions.)

Positive emotions: the more the better. Even the most horrendous life experiences can provide positive feelings and insights. In some circles, this is almost heretical to mention. This is not to say that traumas are a good idea — rather, they have the potential to remind us of the good things in life. Recent studies on expressive writing where the focus is on benefit-finding have documented significant results (Stockdale 2011).

One of the most surprising linguistic findings about expressive writing is that people who use more positive emotions in their writing benefit more from the exercise. We can see positive emotions when words such as *love, caring, funny, joy, beautiful,* and *warmth* are used. If you can use these words even when you are dealing with terrible traumas, you are more likely to notice improvements after writing.

Being able to acknowledge positive emotions when dealing with tragic events is related to work on optimism and benefit-finding (Seligman 2012; Seligman 2011; Fredrickson 2009; Seligman & Csikszentmihalyi 2000). Across an increasing number of studies, people who can see the positive sides of negative experiences have been shown to cope better. Some research even suggests a formula of recalling just three good things to help boost mood (Fredrickson 2009).

This is not to say that you should be some kind of Pollyanna who pretends everything is wonderful. In fact, if you have tried to do this in the past, you have probably learned that it doesn't work. The take-home message from this research is that it is important to acknowledge the bad and look for the good. The degree to which you can do this in your writing is one factor that correlates with improved health.

Constructing a story

Why would humans have evolved so that expressive writing could be emotionally beneficial? The answer can be found in the nature of language and human relationships. Since the beginning of spoken language, people have used words to describe events to others. Part of any description of an event is built around a story or narrative. If I tell you how I got a flat tire on my car, there is a standard way I'll describe the event: the setting of the scene, the occurrence of the unexpected event, my reaction to it, and what happened afterwards.

Stories are an essential part of who we are. They provide a way for us to understand both simple and extremely complicated experiences. Just as we need stories to convey ideas to others, we also need stories to understand things that happen to us. One discussion within the expressive writing world is whether the authors' ability to construct a coherent story around the traumatic experience is one of the major predictors of improved health. There is some interesting evidence for this.

Certain types of words can serve as markers of stories. For example, words such as *cause, effect, because, reason,* and *rationale* suggest that the writer is conveying what may have caused what. Causal reasoning is a way of understanding an event: if I know what caused something, I'll better appreciate when it might occur in the future. Similarly, another class of words called insight words (including words like *understand, realize, know,* and *meaning*) point to the person standing back and trying to formulate a broader understanding of something.

Several studies have shown that people who increase their use of these story-markers, causal words, and insight words tend to show the greatest improvements in physical health after expressive writing (Pennebaker, Mayne, & Francis 1997). It seems that those who start using a relatively low number of these words and but increase their use over the days of writing are putting together a story of their trauma.

In thinking about the phrase "constructing a story," there should be an emphasis on the word *constructing*. Merely having a story to explain a trauma does not predict health improvements. Rather, the person must build or construct a story over the course of writing.

In our own research, it took years for me to appreciate the power of story construction. Oftentimes, someone would write about a traumatic experience, and on their first writing day, they could sew together a perfect story — a clear beginning, middle, and end — a seamless explanation why things happened as they did. I would often be transfixed by these stories because the author appeared so insightful and psychologically healthy. What bothered me, however, was that very few of these people showed any benefits from writing. It's now clear that they *already had* a story. Perhaps these people should have been writing about something else. Writing seems most beneficial when you are trying to make sense of an event you don't yet understand.

The idea of constructing a story is similar to that of psychological growth. If you found yourself writing about the same trauma in the same way over the four-day writing exercise, it is not likely that writing was particularly beneficial for you. Expressive writing, like psychotherapy or even a human relationship, must exhibit change over time to be healthy.

Changing perspectives

As a trauma or emotional upheaval unfolds, we tend to look at it from our own perspective. Only with time are we able to begin to appreciate what others were thinking, feeling, and seeing during the same period. Recent linguistic research is now finding that the ability to see an upheaval from different perspectives may be particularly beneficial (Campbell & Pennebaker 2003).

The key to perspectives comes from an unlikely source: pronouns. Remember pronouns from high school? *I, you, he, she, it, we, they, me, my,* and so on. It turns out that pronouns are extremely important in understanding how we write (Pennebaker 2011). For example, if you use a high number of first person singular pronouns (*I, me, my, mine, myself*), you are emphasizing your personal perspective, and you may also be self-focused. This is often good when writing about traumatic experiences. But the research indicates that it is healthy to write about other people as well.

Go back to your four days of writing. You might even go through and circle the first person singular pronouns. Are you using these pronouns at roughly the same rate from day to day in your writing? People tend to benefit more from writing if their rates of first person singular pronouns change a great deal from one day to the next. In fact, if your rates are very similar from day to day, you are less likely to show health improvements.

Changes in pronoun use suggest changes in perspective. When dealing with something as massive as a trauma, it is important to see it from several different angles. No perspective is better or more valid than others; instead, it's important to get a sense of the many dimensions of the trauma you have experienced.

Putting It All Together

You might think it peculiar that I'm telling you about the secrets of healthy writing in Chapter 4. Why, you ask, didn't you mention these gems before the four-day writing exercise? The answer is simple. If you knew that you should use a high number of positive and a moderate number of negative emotion words, that you had to construct a story, and that you should bounce around in your use of pronouns, you would have been thinking about the words themselves rather than your traumatic experience.

In looking back at your writing, you may have noticed that you naturally wrote in most of the ways that have been found to be healthy. Unfortunately, other writing techniques probably require some practice to become more natural. And that's why there are more chapters in this book.

I hope that the four-day writing exercise was extremely beneficial for you — so much so that you don't feel like writing anymore, at least not at this time in your life. If that *is* how you feel, then slowly put the book down and walk quietly away. To be honest, that is exactly what I would do.

My coauthor, John, has a different perspective. He writes every day and gets great value from it. He would suggest that even if the four-day writing exercise was wonderfully helpful, you should keep reading this book and explore additional writing methods.

We both believe that if the four-day writing method was not valuable, it might be a good idea to try some additional strategies to see if one might match your needs or interests better. In either case, the following chapters have been designed as a series of writing exercises to help expand your horizon of writing.

PART II

Experimenting with Writing

This above all: to thine ownself be true,
And it must follow, as the night the day,
Thou canst not then be false to any man.
                    — *William Shakespeare (from Hamlet)*

There is no absolute right way to disclose traumatic experiences. The four-day writing exercise in Chapter 3 is the most rigorously tested method available. Although it works in a large percentage of people in reducing the unwanted effects of emotional upheavals, the four-day technique is far from perfect. Think of the four-day writing technique as your basic, no-frills, stripped-down floor model. Researchers are currently studying other writing strategies that, on occasion, have boosted the power of expressive writing. Some methods have been quite successful for some people, but not for others.

In the following sections, Jamie Pennebaker describes several experimental methods. The exercises are not introduced in any particular order. Rather, they represent a broad spectrum of potentially valuable ways of writing for you to experiment with.

For most techniques, a brief ten-minute writing exercise is suggested. Some exercises are recommended to last only five minutes and others as long as twenty minutes. These relatively brief exercises are designed to give you a taste of a particular approach. If it helps, use a clock to make sure you write for the minimum recommended time. If you find that these techniques are helpful or in some way satisfy your creative urges, expand your writing beyond the recommended minimum. In fact, don't feel compelled to use a clock at all if you think it might constrict you. Also, you might try the same exercises several days in a row.

For each of the exercises, first read about them and see if they make sense to you. You are the expert on you. Try the exercises and discard those methods that don't work. Also, invent your own methods and styles of writing.

5

Writing to Break Mental Blocks

It's not uncommon to plan on writing about an emotional event and end up staring at a blank piece of paper or computer screen. You may know the feeling. You have a great deal to say but don't know where to start. Or you may begin writing, but everything you write sounds false, stilted, or just plain stupid.

One reason people develop mental blocks about writing is that they are often too self-critical. That little censor in their head is telling them that they need to write artistically or perfectly. That censor may be your high school English teacher, a parent, or someone you want to impress. To start expressive or therapeutic writing, you must dispense with the censor and give yourself permission to write anything.

Stream of Consciousness Writing

One tried and true method of writing is called stream of consciousness writing: simply place your thoughts and feelings on paper as they occur. The only rule is that you write continuously. Don't try to censor yourself. Before reading about it in any detail, try it out.

Simply begin writing. You can use your e-reader's note-taking feature, your journal, or loose-leaf paper. Write in a stream of consciousness way for ten minutes or until approximately two writing pages are filled. In your writing, simply track your thoughts and feelings as they occur. Just write what you are thinking about, what you are feeling, hearing, smelling, or noticing. It is important that your writing simply follows your stream of thought. Don't worry about spelling, grammar, or sentence structure. Remember that this writing is for you alone and that you can destroy it when you are finished. Just begin writing and don't stop.

William James, an early founder of modern psychology, was one of the first people to explore the idea of stream of consciousness. He believed our stream of consciousness revealed a great deal about us. He made four general observations:

1. Every thought is ultimately personal. We know what the thought means, but others may not. In a sense, then, every thought you write has meaning to you.

2. Thoughts are sensibly continuous (like a stream, thought one is related to thought two and thought two is related to thought three — but thought three may not be related to thought one). In other words, thoughts don't appear randomly, although they may appear to. Look over your writing and explore your transitions. Why did one thought lead to the next one?

3. We can consciously think of only one thing at a time. Even though our brains may be detecting and analyzing sights, sounds, hunger pangs, and bittersweet memories of last night — all at the same time — we can be consciously aware of only one of these thoughts or perceptions at any given instant.

4. It is meaningful to explore both what we think about and what we actively *don't* think about. At some level, our mind chooses

where our stream of thought goes. In your own writing, did you consciously choose to avoid a topic? Or subtly move your thinking (or typing) in a direction that it would not normally have gone?

Topical Stream of Consciousness Writing

Stream of consciousness writing can be used in many ways. If you are blocked about writing on a particular topic, you can focus your writing on it. This topic could be a particular emotional issue, a boring report for your job, or an important writing sample that people will ultimately evaluate. If you don't have problems writing about something, you can skip this section. But if there is a particular issue or project that you simply can't start, this may help.

Topical stream of consciousness writing uses the same principles as the stream of consciousness writing that you used at the beginning of this chapter. The only difference is that you should write *about the topic.* Some possible prompts to get you going:

* *I'm sitting here unable to write about _____. Why am I having trouble writing about this?*
* *Thinking about this topic brings up a number of disconnected thoughts, including ...*
* *In my life, there have been other times that I have been blocked about writing. How is this time similar? What is it about me that won't let me get started?*
* *This topic is arousing a lot of emotions in me. Some of these emotions include...*

You can see the idea behind these prompts. Merely addressing the problem of writing is a first step in getting past a writing block. Indeed, several recent studies have suggested that simply labeling the problem and our feelings associated with it can help. Once we have a better understanding of the factors holding us back from writing, we can move forward.

Topical stream of consciousness writing can sometimes be thought of as a priming-the-pump method. Once you start writing about why you are having trouble writing about the topic, ideas about the topic start flowing out. If this happens, go with it. You can always erase your stream of consciousness meanderings later (if this is for a report at work).

As a simple exercise, why not try out the topical stream of consciousness writing? Here are the basic instructions:

For the next ten minutes, write about that issue that you are having trouble writing about. Write continuously without worrying about spelling or grammar. You might start by using one of the prompts above.

Semi-Automatic Writing

If you are interested in the occult world, you may have heard of automatic writing. The idea is that people can put themselves into a passive mental state and write at the same time. Some people then report that their hands begin writing automatically. This "automatic writing" is often attributed to spirits, angels, demons, aliens, or some other paranormal phenomenon. A generation of psychological research has shown that these possession-like feelings are simple illusions (Wegner 2002).

What is interesting about the automatic writing phenomenon is that you can use it to turn off your mind's censor. If something is bothering you and you're not sure what it is, a form of automatic writing may be useful. Let's not call it automatic writing, however. How about semi-automatic writing? By the way, if you have been abducted by aliens, are a firm believer in demonic possession, or think that alien forces are controlling your thoughts and behaviors, skip this section.

Semi-automatic writing can work using either a computer or with handwriting. The only rule: don't look at what you're writing. For a computer, simply turn off the monitor. For handwriting, get a cloth or towel and drape it over your writing hand and paper. You can also simply shut your eyes or look in another direction. Before you begin writing, try to clear your mind. You might focus on your breathing, your emotions, or some object.

Once your attention is elsewhere, begin writing. Don't pay conscious attention to what you are writing. If you're typing, you will undoubtedly make typographical errors. If you're writing by hand, you won't always write within the lines. Don't worry about it. Just let yourself write without paying attention to the writing process itself.

Try writing this way for a solid ten minutes.

When you're finished, read what you have written. Sometimes you'll see a jumble of words and letters. Other times you may see yourself addressing important issues. Keep in mind that there is no magic in this strategy. It's simply a way for you to touch on topics that you may be avoiding or not deeply aware of. Indeed, some people have suggested that the results of semi-automatic writing are a little like dreams. They give us a glimpse of hidden issues that are bothering us.

6

Writing to Appreciate the Good in a Sometimes Bad World

Traumatic experiences have the potential to touch every part of our lives — in both good and bad ways. After tragedies, for example, people often report a stronger sense of their social connections and a rediscovered sense of meaning in their lives.

Analyses of writing samples have consistently found that people who can express positive emotions while writing about tragic events tend to benefit most from expressive writing. In recent years, research in positive psychology has shown that recalling and expressing positive feelings has healthful benefits.

Let's be clear from the outset. If you have experienced a trauma, friends may have told you a number of simple, stupid-sounding, optimistic things like:

"In a few years you will look back at this and laugh."

No, you probably won't.

"Look on the good side, at least [fill in ridiculous platitude here]."

There may not be a good side worth looking at — now or ever.

"Hey, cheer up!"

Hey, drop dead.

People often want you to be happy after a trauma because your pain is difficult for *them* to deal with. If you could put on a chipper, upbeat face, they would be far more comfortable. But this false happiness is not a true positive emotion. This chapter's exercises may be helpful in encouraging you to draw on your deeper reservoirs of love, meaning, and contentment. No false grins or chirpy expressions are expected (or wanted).

Acknowledging and Expressing Positive Emotion

In 1989, two psychologists, Camille Wortman and Roxanne Silver, published a groundbreaking article entitled "Myths of coping with loss." Drawing on a large number of sound studies, the authors pointed out that not everyone gets depressed after the death of a spouse or child. In fact, almost half of those who have experienced a major loss are healthy and happy soon afterwards. Some psychologists were upset to learn that people could actually be happy and well-adjusted in the face of an overwhelming personal trauma. It somehow seemed socially unacceptable and counter to common wisdom.

As discussed in Chapter 4, the ability to use positive emotion words when writing about a traumatic experience predicts better health after the writing exercise. Some of the hundreds of positive emotion words include:

love	joy	happy	caring	pretty
nice	peace	good	laughter	strong
dignity	trust	courageous	accepting	calm
fun	gentle	humor	inspiring	kiss
perfect	proud	contented	secure	satisfied
glad	merry	romantic	thankful	easy

For some people, using positive emotion words when writing about trauma requires practice. With your preferred method or writing your thoughts and feelings, try writing about a negative experience for ten minutes using as many positive emotion words as possible. You can use as many negative emotion words as you need to as well. All the time, try to be honest about the experience. In other words, don't lie to yourself and write that something was joyful when it wasn't.

When selecting a negative event, start with something only slightly negative. Don't jump into a massive trauma. The goal here is to practice using both positive emotion words and, when needed, negative emotion words. In fact, if you can use, say, "not calm" instead of "worried," you will have used one of the positive emotion words. (Studies suggest that using "not happy" is better for your health than using "sad.")

So, here we go. For the next ten minutes, write continuously about a negative experience. Describe what happened, how you felt then and now, and anything else relevant. Try to use as many positive emotions words as you can while at the same time staying true to your experience. Write continuously without stopping.

If my calculations are correct, the last ten minutes of writing were more difficult than you thought. Read over what you just wrote and see where you used positive emotion versus negative emotion words. Where were you honest with yourself and where were you not? In retrospect, how could you have used more positive emotion words in describing the event and its aftermath?

Let's try this exercise one more time. This time, don't look at the positive emotion word list. Write about the same experience for ten minutes and think where the occasional positive feeling might bubble up.

Now that you have completed both writing exercises, reflect on how you felt after each one. Most people feel far more comfortable and satisfied after the second exercise than they did after the first. Pay attention to how you use words when talking or writing about upheavals in your life. Acknowledge and express positive feelings when you can.

Writing to Find Benefit

Another approach to positive emotions is to actively look for the benefits that may come as a result of a trauma or emotional upheaval. Several research teams have found that people who can find meaning or other benefits in misfortune cope much better with traumas than people who can't. Some expressive writing studies explicitly asked people to write about their traumas in a way that emphasized their positive experience. For many people, this benefit-finding writing perspective was beneficial.

For this next exercise, try your hand at benefit-finding writing. Think of an emotional upheaval or other negative experience in your past. For the next ten minutes, briefly describe the event and then write about any benefits that came from it, such as a greater understanding of yourself and others, or a change in the direction of your life that may have avoided more heartache or that led to happiness or growth. In your writing, be honest and open with yourself.

Broaching Forgiveness

Forgive and forget. There is a kernel of truth to this adage. Being able to say "I forgive you" or, if you are the wrongdoer, "Please forgive me" can be a significant step in the healing process. Many times, asking for or granting forgiveness is not possible. Perhaps the other person is not available or does not want to deal with you. Other times, merely talking to another person about an upsetting experience will only open old wounds that can't be healed. Especially when there are social barriers like these to forgiveness, writing about a past injustice can be helpful.

Granting forgiveness when you have been the victim

For many people, forgiving others for upending their lives can be an almost impossible task. Forgiving the perpetrator of a terrible event implies letting them get away with an injustice. *Not* forgiving, however, implies the continuation of anger and bitterness. And although we rarely admit it, truly hating or resenting another person can be satisfying. Forgiveness, then, is potentially disrupting. The real payoff, however, is that forgiving can increase the odds that you can get on with your life.

A granting-forgiveness exercise. This is a writing exercise for you if you have suffered an injustice as a result of another person *and* you feel you could forgive them. Although this exercise is designed to last only ten minutes, consider writing for twenty minutes per day for three to four consecutive days if you have a serious forgiveness issue to deal with.

Before writing, think about a specific situation in which you were treated badly by another. Recall how you felt before, during, and after the event. More important, imagine how the other person might have felt. Why do you think the person felt that way? Don't demonize the other person — she or he is a human just like you, with fears, insecurities, and stories of his or her own.

For the next ten minutes, write about your deepest emotions and thoughts about this event. Briefly mention what led up to the event. Focus more on the person who was responsible for what happened. What do you think was going on in his or her life at the time? How do you think the person felt afterwards? What will it take for you to forgive what was done? If you feel as though you can forgive the person, do so on paper. Explore what being able to forgive means to you and to the other person. As always, write continuously and write in an uncensored manner — plan that no one else will see your writing.

Asking for forgiveness when you have caused suffering

Just as we have all been victims at some points in our lives, we have also caused suffering in others — either intentionally or accidentally. Although asking forgiveness via writing is a socially isolated act, it can be of value psychologically. More than anything, it forces writers to acknowledge their hand in causing another's unhappiness.

Before writing, spend some time thinking about something you have done in the past that caused someone else emotional pain. Think carefully of what led up to the event, what was going on in your mind at the time, and how you felt afterwards. Imagine how the other person felt and what he or she may have thought. Consider also how your action may have indirectly affected the other person's family or friends. Finally, think about how you might have felt and behaved if the same event had happened to you.

As with the granting-forgiveness exercise, use the following writing task as an experiment. If you have an issue that is central to who you are, then consider writing for twenty minutes a day for three to four consecutive days with the same general instructions. In addition, you may have more than one person to whom you would like to say "I'm sorry." Try the ten-minute-asking-for-forgiveness exercise for those most relevant to your life.

For the next ten minutes, briefly describe what happened and what role you played in causing pain for another person. Don't use your writing to justify your actions. Rather, focus on the other person's feelings and thoughts. If you can, express your sorrow for this event. You might write out an apology to the other person as if she or he were going to read it. Explore the possibility of what it would take to make amends with this person and their friends and family now. As always, write continuously and write in an uncensored manner — plan that no one else will see your writing.

7

Writing and Editing Your Story

As we note in Chapter 1, research dealing with expressive writing suggests that people are most likely to benefit from writing about a trauma if they can build a coherent story of their experience. The operative word is *building* a story — not just *having* one. One problem: deciding what a good story is. What may be good for one person may be superficial or deluded for another.

Despite the many disagreements about what constitutes a coherent story, most people agree on some basic elements. Whether you are writing a novel or merely about a personal trauma, the following features are generally included:

A description of the setting. When and where did the event occur? What was going on at the time?

A sense of the main characters. Who was involved and what were they doing? What were they thinking and feeling? What were you doing, thinking, and feeling prior to the event?

A clear description of the event or upheaval. What triggered the event and what exactly happened? How did you react as it was unfolding?

The immediate and long-term consequences. What happened as a result of the event? How did this upheaval influence your life and the lives of others? How did the event shape your current situation and emotional state?

The meaning of the story. Why are you telling this story to yourself or others? Why has it had such an effect on you? What have you learned as a result of your experience?

Not all good stories include all of these features. In fact, according to the expressive writing research, some of the best and most helpful narratives have started with glaring holes. When they began writing, participants often didn't know exactly what happened, what the real consequences were, or what it meant. However, over the days of writing, they began to build a more coherent and meaningful story that made sense to them.

A Simple Story Construction Exercise

To illustrate the steps in constructing a meaningful story, this exercise is a two-step process. Rather than writing about a massive upheaval in your life, think about an upsetting or confusing event that has happened to you recently. Maybe a fight with a family member or friend, or perhaps an unexpected conflict at work. Ideally, this event should be something you have thought about a few times in the last couple of days. Have an event in mind? Good.

Step One: Just Write

Without thinking or censoring your thoughts, write for no more than ten minutes about what happened. Just spit it out on paper. Don't try to impose any kind of structure on the event. No need to analyze it. Just write.

Now that you have finished, go back and read what you have written. In all likelihood, your writing was much less random than you thought. You probably put things together in a surprisingly organized way. As you read it, however, you will probably notice that you left some important things out, and that you didn't address certain thoughts and emotions.

Before proceeding to the next step, give yourself some time — even a few minutes — to reconsider this event. When you return, your goal will be to write about the same event while imposing more structure on it. That is, you will be asked to include information on the setting, characters, the event itself, consequences, and the meaning of it as though you were telling the story to someone else. Think about this for a few minutes.

Step Two: Constructing a Story

Humans in all cultures around the world create stories in part to convey complex ideas and emotions to others in organized and simple ways. The event you wrote about in Step One was probably moderately complex. If you were concerned with detail, you could probably have stretched the event to five or ten pages — maybe into a novel that even you wouldn't have wanted to read. Stories are also created because they allow us to summarize complex events into smaller packages.

Consider the elements of a good and coherent story. Focus especially on the event, its consequences, and its meaning. For this phase of the exercise, rewrite the event that you addressed in Step One. This time, however, imagine you are telling the event to a stranger you will never see again. In your story, be a good and honest storyteller. Once you begin writing, do not look at your original writing sample. Try to write your story in ten minutes, but take more time if you need it.

When you have completed Step Two, go back and compare your two stories. How have they changed? How do you feel about the event itself now that you have addressed it twice? Most people find that the second writing exercise was less exciting to write but somehow got them past the event better. The second writing experience tends to force structure on the upsetting event that wasn't there before. In fact, you might now consider the entire episode a bit tedious. Maybe you want to move on to other issues in your life. And that is precisely the point of writing about the event two times.

Rewriting and Editing Your Traumatic Experience

The point of the simple story construction exercise was to stimulate your thinking about the idea that personal traumas are a form of story. If you are able to transform a chaotic personal upheaval into an honest and coherent story, you are more likely to be able to move past the event.

Just as you can use the story construction process on relatively minor upheavals, you can use it on major traumas as well. There are some important differences, however. A major personal trauma can be a story in itself. It can also loom so large in your life that it can create multiple mini-stories. A trauma, then, has the potential to grow into a novel where one event cascades into others, each one with its own plot and meaning.

To apply the story construction process to your own major upheaval, start by using the writing instructions in Chapter 3. Once you have completed the Chapter 3 writing, you can use that experience as the base for the following exercises. Two overlapping techniques are outlined.

The first encourages you to reconsider your trauma as a broad story using all of the elements of a classic story. The second technique suggests ways to go back and edit your trauma narrative. Try this broad rewriting and editing when you have plenty of time.

Working Your Trauma into a Story

If you kept your writing from Chapter 3, go back and read it. If not, try to reconstruct what you wrote. It is likely that your writing dealt with several issues that may have really been more than one emotional upheaval. For the purpose of this exercise, try to focus on what you believe to be the most central event or issue for you.

Read over and think about your expressive writing. Consider the essential aspects of it. In your original writing, you probably found yourself dealing with tangential issues or even topics that distracted you from what you really needed to write about. As you read and think about this trauma, consider how you can make this experience an organized and meaningful story. As always, this story is for you and you alone — which means it needs to be honest in every way.

For this exercise, write for a minimum of twenty minutes on a single occasion. You may find that a single writing session for this task is impossible. If you need to write more, then do it. Each person's story is very different. Some can boil their upheaval down to a simple theme and tie up the main points in ten minutes. Others will write for several days.

Before you begin writing, review the essential elements of a good story: setting, characters, a description of the event, and the event's immediate and long-term consequences. Most importantly, focus on the meaning of the event. It wouldn't hurt to also consider the findings of Chapter 5 — remember that emphasizing the positive or potential benefits of an unwanted experience can yield better health.

Basic instructions. For the next twenty minutes, work your traumatic experience into a story with a clear beginning, middle, and end. Describe the experience and how it has affected you and others. What has this event meant for you? In your writing, express your emotions freely and be honest with yourself. Once you begin writing, write continuously the entire twenty minutes. If your story goes in a direction you didn't anticipate, follow your heart. You can always write again tomorrow.

As always, this writing is for you alone. Don't worry about spelling, grammar, or sentence structure.

Many people find it difficult to make a coherent story about an overwhelming event — especially on their first try. If this was your experience, consider writing about the same event again. Each time you write, however, try to change your orientation and thinking. Work to make the event more organized and structured. If you feel it is warranted, write the story over and over again until you are bored with it. Getting bored with your own trauma, by the way, is a sign of progress. The boredom is a signal from your brain telling you to get on with your life.

The possible power of editing and reworking your writing

We now come to a debatable topic. Several people I deeply respect believe that editing and rewriting your expressive writing is both powerful and healthy. Other people just don't like to do it. This is clearly an issue of personal taste. Read the idea behind it and try it. If you find rewriting meaningful, experiment more with it on your own.

In writing about a trauma, you may struggle to know what features of the trauma are most important. Sometimes you think one aspect may have changed your life, but on reflection, you realize that something else was far more significant. When you go back and edit your expressive writings, you can remake your own history with the benefit of hindsight.

This is not to say you are reinventing your trauma. Rather, extensive editing and rewriting of your story helps you focus on what is most relevant to your life right now.

If you have done most of the writing exercises in earlier chapters, you have several possible writing samples to work with. Perhaps the most relevant is either the expressive writing exercise in Chapter 3 or the trauma-into-a-story exercise you just completed. You can use either writing, but for the purpose of this exercise, let's use your trauma-into-a-story exercise.

Basic instructions. The purpose of this exercise is to rewrite and edit your sample into a more organized, honest, and coherent story. Unlike every other writing exercise, with this one, you should collaborate with your mind's "censor." That is, you should look at the logical flow of your writing, your writing style, and what you intend to say. Your goal is to make this a better story in every way.

As a first step, simply make a neat copy of the story — perhaps copy it onto a computer or into a notebook. Correct any misspellings or awkward sentences. Be honest with yourself in reporting on the feelings and thoughts. Gradually work on the structure of the essay. You may have to work on it at a sentence-by-sentence level. Does each idea follow in a meaningful and logical way?

After you have worked on it awhile, take some time away — several minutes, hours, or even days. When you return, read it and make more changes. This is a story for yourself that should express your deepest emotions and thoughts in an open and honest way. It should also be a story with a clear beginning, middle, and end. Above all, your story should have a point to it. Why are you telling this story? What benefits has this experience brought to you?

If it looks as if this editing process will take a long time, give yourself a deadline. If you find that you are becoming obsessed with this project, stop. The purpose of this writing exercise is for you to work through the trauma — not to wrap yourself into it. If you can't seem to find any meaning in the event no matter how hard you look, then admit it and walk away. Some experiences in life simply may not have any meaning or value.

As a final note, people vary tremendously in what they consider to be satisfying and meaningful stories. Trust your own instincts in your writing. If, after writing something, you feel as though you have gained benefit from it even though most other people would view it as a jumbled mess, then pat yourself on the back. You have succeeded.

8

Writing to Change Perspectives

Some of the most exciting research discoveries concern the role of perspective in expressive writing. People who benefit most from writing about traumas change how they focus on a trauma from day to day. One day, for example, they may focus primarily on their own feelings and experiences; on other days they might talk about the thoughts and feelings of others who have been involved in the trauma.

Because this research is very new, it is hard to know why changing your perspective is related to improved health. Maybe if you can look at an upsetting event from different angles, you are able to stand back from it. In other words, the ability to adopt alternative perspectives both requires and reflects a certain detachment.

There have been some preliminary studies where people have been asked to try to change their perspectives while writing about personal upheavals (Andersson & Conley 2013; Campbell & Pennebaker 2003; Seih, Chung, & Pennebaker 2011). The initial results are promising, although some people clearly enjoy switching perspectives more than others. Two perspective-changing exercises are described in this chapter: writing from the third-person perspective and writing flexibly with pronouns. Try them out and see if you find them valuable.

Writing from the Third-Person Perspective

Many novelists struggle with the voice (point-of-view) of their main character. What are the implications if the story begins with a first-person versus a third-person perspective? Consider the first two sentences of a trauma essay:

First-person voice: When I was seventeen, my father left home. I was stuck in a family war between my sister and mother. They hated each other and tried to pull me into their battles. Even writing about it brings up the pain and sadness I always felt in our house.

Third-person voice: When he was seventeen, his father left home. He was stuck in a family war between his sister and mother. The two hated each other and tried to pull him into their battles. Even writing about it brings up the pain and sadness he always felt in their house.

Changing the perspective from first person (I, me, our) to third person (he, him, they) subtly alters the tone of the story. The third-person view is more distanced, and from the reader's view, safer. It is not uncommon for people who have lived through a truly massive trauma (such as torture) to initially describe the experience in the third person. Only when they begin to feel more comfortable talking about it will they begin to talk in the first person.

Two third-person writing exercises are suggested. The first one, dealing with a recent problem or conflict, is for you to practice with. Once you feel comfortable using third person, try the second exercise and write about a feature of the trauma or emotional upheaval most relevant to your life.

Brief Perspective-Switching Writing

Think of an event, conflict, or other issue that you have been dealing with lately. This should not be a massive trauma — rather, choose something that you would label as a mere annoyance. As outlined below, your goal is to write about this experience on two occasions, each time for about ten minutes. Give yourself a break of at least a few minutes between the two writing exercises.

Writing in the first person. These should be familiar instructions. For the next ten minutes, describe your emotions and thoughts about a recent event that you have been thinking or worrying about. Describe things from your normal first-person perspective — the "I" voice. In your writing, describe the event and your reactions to it. You may link it to other things in your past or present. Once you begin, write continuously for the entire ten minutes.

Writing in the third person. Before beginning to write on this exercise, look back and read what you wrote as part of the first-person instructions. For the next ten minutes, write about the same general issue, but this time use third-person voice. If you are a female, replace your normal "I" with "she." Use "he" if you are a male. In other words, write about the actions and emotions of the main character (who is you) as though you were observing everything as an outsider. Try to include the same basic information that you included initially.

When you've completed the third-person writing, stand back and evaluate how writing in this way felt compared with your normal first-person writing. Many people report mixed feelings when they first try it — that it just doesn't feel natural. This is an issue of practice. The more you use third-person perspective in your writing, the more comfortable it will feel.

Before giving up on the third-person approach, try this exercise again later when you're writing on another topic. Instead of starting with first person and then switching to third person, go in the reverse order. That is, first describe the event from the distanced third person and then write a second time in first person.

Addressing your trauma from the third-person perspective

The brief perspective-switching exercise was really a way of practicing third-person writing. The true value of writing in the third person is in dealing with particularly powerful emotional upheavals. If you continue to be haunted by a trauma or upheaval, you may find writing in the third-person perspective to be beneficial. As with all exercises, try it out and see if is meaningful for you.

For this exercise, write about an emotional upheaval that dominates your thoughts and feelings. In your writing, try to let go and explore your very deepest emotions and thoughts about it. Instead of referring to this trauma as "my experience" or "my feelings," write entirely in the third person as if you were an observer reporting on your own experience. What happened to this person? What led up to the event? How did the person react and why? How were other people affected? How does the other person feel now? What meaning can you draw from this person's experience?

Write continuously during the entire twenty minutes and maintain the third-person perspective. If you slip into first person, mark it out and change what you have written into third person. Remember that this writing is for you alone.

Reflecting on third-person writing. Third-person writing can be a powerful tool in dealing with highly charged emotional events. Oftentimes, those emotions and experiences that are the most raw and painful can best be dealt with by a more detached voice. With repeated telling, you can begin to move to the more natural first person. This exercise should be viewed as a first step. If it was helpful, try using third-person for other assignments. The ability to use both first- and third-person perspectives can help maintain an emotional flexibility in dealing with any upheavals that may come your way.

Writing Flexibly with Pronouns

Pronouns? Would you ever have thought you would read a book that extolled the virtue of pronouns — or any part of speech, for that matter? As noted in Chapter 4, pronouns may actually be critically important in understanding the power of expressive writing.

Interestingly, this was an accidental discovery. Researchers studying writing samples from old experiments found that people who changed how they used pronouns from one writing day to the next had better health in subsequent months. Those who used pronouns in the same ways day after day didn't improve.

A closer look indicates that the central distinction is between the word "I" and all other pronouns (you, they, me, we, and so on). If the person uses the word "I" a great deal on one day and then other pronouns on the next day, that's good. Similarly, using other pronouns on one day (but not much "I") and then a great deal of "I" on the next is also good.

Using pronouns the same way across all days is associated with only minor health improvements following the writing intervention.

These may be extremely important results. Pronouns themselves are not making people healthy or sick, of course. Instead, the pronouns reflect how people think about traumatic experiences. If people write about a given trauma several days in a row and always use the same pronouns, their thinking process is probably rigid. Maybe they are talking about their own perspective every day; maybe they are only focusing on someone else. The writers who benefit, however, are flipping perspectives day to day. One day, the writer may be describing another's actions and emotions; the next day, the focus may be the writer's own actions and feelings.

It's tempting to set up a writing exercise where you are asked to use pronouns from List A on the first day of writing and pronouns from List B on the next day. Unfortunately, this approach won't work. People would look so often at the word lists while trying to use the right pronouns that they would forget what they are writing about. A better approach is to think about perspectives. Focusing on different people (while still including yourself) from essay to essay may cause the pronouns to follow.

Virtually all personal upheavals are social. A trauma may happen to just you, but it usually affects others directly or indirectly. In all likelihood, another person was involved in the trauma. The reason we use pronouns at such high rates when writing about traumas is because we need to talk about both ourselves and the other people.

In this writing exercise, try describing an emotionally important event from several perspectives. Plan for this exercise to last about twenty minutes, devoting five minutes to each of four perspectives. In the first five-minute period, lay out what happened, who was involved, and what is happening now. The second period should focus exclusively on your perspective, feelings, and actions. The third writing period should deal with one or more of the other people in this story. In the final writing period, stand back and try to integrate all the perspectives. For this exercise, simply move from one writing instruction to the next without stopping.

Perspective One: The Big Picture

For the next five minutes, write continuously about an emotional upheaval that is important to your life. In your writing, mention what happened and who was involved. How did you and others react to this event, and how is it affecting all of you now? As soon as you are finished with this section, continue with the instructions for Perspective Two.

Perspective Two: I, me, and my

For the next five minutes, write about the same emotional upheaval but focus exclusively on *your* perspective. What did *you* think, feel, and react? How have *your* behaviors affected others? What would *you* like others to know about *your* situation? Write continuously and honestly. When you are finished, continue to Perspective Three.

Perspective Three: The Other People

You are halfway finished with this exercise. For the next five minutes, write about the same general trauma but focus on the role of another person or group. What was and is going on in their minds? What did they do and feel? What do you think they would like others to know about their perspective? Try to look into their hearts and assume that they are complicated human beings, just as you are. Write continuously and, when finished, move onto Perspective Four.

Perspective Four: Another Big Picture.

Before you begin writing, look back at what you have written so far. Have you been honest with yourself and about the other people? For this last five-minute writing period, again tell the story of this trauma. Take a broad perspective. What value or meaning can you and others draw from this experience? Write continuously the entire time.

The point of this last exercise was to get you to think about adopting multiple perspectives in dealing with a complex emotional event. Go back and look at your use of pronouns from perspective to perspective. Ideally, you changed a great deal in the percentage of "I" words. If the number of "I" words was similar across all four writings, ask yourself why this was the case. It might be beneficial to try this assignment again and consciously try to change your pronouns to force a perspective change.

If you found this exercise helpful, consider writing about other upheavals in your life. Write about each upheaval on multiple occasions, adopting a slightly different perspective each time. As you become adept at viewing the same upheaval from different directions, you will also find yourself getting more and more detached from the event.

9

Writing in Different Contexts

The context of your writing — when and where you write — likely influences *what* you write. Potential places, audiences, and times are suggested in this chapter, but experiment with your own writing sessions to devise the best contexts for your writing.

Some situations may make you feel defensive, while others allow you to be vulnerable. Although very little solid research has been conducted on writing context, a smattering of findings suggest that changes in the time and place of writing can affect people's orientation to an emotional upheaval. This chapter requires you to conduct your own small experiments. In reading this chapter, follow your own instincts. Be playful and scientific at the same time. As always, embrace what works and discard what doesn't.

Locations and Settings

Where you are affects how you think. If you walk by a restaurant, you often can't help but think of food. The kind of music you hear in a grocery story can influence what you buy. A recent study, for example, found that if people heard Italian music in a wine shop, they were more likely to buy Italian wine. It follows, then, that where you write can subtly affect the memories and emotions that bubble to the surface.

Writing settings can vary along an infinite number of dimensions. Rather than a list of places to write, four simple contexts for writing will be suggested. Try them and see what happens.

Writing to Boost Self-focus with Mirrors

When we see our reflection or hear our own voice, we automatically become more self-attentive. Beginning in the 1970s, a stunning number of experiments found that when people were put in front of a mirror, they became more honest and aware of who they were. Although the effects were striking, they were subtle. People didn't have any idea that the mirrors were affecting them (Wicklund 1979). Is it possible that writing in the presence of a mirror can influence your writing? In a recent test of this idea, we found that for some people, writing in front of a mirror was a particularly powerful experience. Try it out.

If you are writing by hand, on a laptop computer, or an e-reader, find a place with a large mirror. The best setting would be in front of a mirror that reflects your face or — better yet — your entire body. If you are writing on a stationary computer, bring a mirror next to you — even just a hand-held mirror. Your general writing assignment will be to explore an emotionally important issue in your life and how it relates to who you are.

Basic instructions. Look at yourself in the mirror. Gaze into your own eyes. Look at your face. See yourself as others see you and as you see yourself. While looking at your image, think about a significant personal issue and how it relates to where you are in your life, your connections to others, and who you really are. After closely examining yourself in the mirror for several minutes, begin writing.

Write continuously for a minimum of ten minutes. Every now and then, look back at your reflection. Be honest with yourself.

When you have finished this assignment, review what you have written. Did you find this exercise valuable? If so, write about other significant emotional experiences in this way as well.

Finding a safe and peaceful context

People often disclose extremely personal stories when they feel the most secure. The confession in person or through prayer in a house of worship, talking to a close friend under the summer stars, or even confiding in a therapist's office are examples of places we can let down our defenses. For this exercise, your goal is to find a setting where you normally feel safe to reveal yourself. Ideally, it should be a place where you generally don't write, away from reminders of your everyday life.

Go to a location where you feel particularly secure. It could be outside at a park or in the woods, in an unused classroom, a church, a library, an old friend's house, or even a bench inside a shopping area or coffee shop. Before you begin writing, you must relax and appreciate your environment. Draw on the feelings of familiarity and connections with your past and with other people. If you have chosen a spiritual setting, consider offering a silent prayer.

Writing instructions. Write for at least ten minutes about an important experience in your past. Before writing, however, focus on your feelings of security and peace linked to the situation you are in. Think how this past experience connects with who you are now. In your writing, explore your emotions and thoughts about this past experience. Write continuously without censoring yourself.

At first, it can be difficult to adjust to a new situation when writing. If this experience was valuable, return to this setting and address deeper, more significant issues. Even if this was not a particularly helpful exercise, consider trying other novel environments. You might look specifically for places that touch different parts of your past: spiritual, home, early childhood, school, or those unique places that only you might associate with safety, honesty, and trust.

Using symbols of the past

Different people using this book have experienced vastly different types of traumatic experiences. For some, this exercise may be inappropriate or too painful. For others, it may be ideally suited to confronting the past. Remembering the Flip-Out Rule, use your own judgment about whether this exercise could be helpful for you.

Growing scientific evidence suggests that people who have experienced traumas in the past can benefit from re-exposing themselves to painful memories of the event. This technique — called flooding, exposure, or implosive therapy — has been used in treating the effects of rape and other violent abuse as well as crippling fears resulting from other traumatic incidents. If your symptoms from a trauma are particularly troublesome, do seek the help of a psychotherapist. However, if you feel you can benefit from a diluted form of exposure, then try the following writing exercise.

For this twenty-minute exercise, you will write about an emotional upheaval that is associated with a particular location, person, or even a smell. Choose a location for your writing that you typically don't use to write — perhaps a garage, the library, even a bathroom. Your task: bring reminders or symbols of the upheaval together in the location you will write in. These reminders could be pictures, letters, clothing — almost anything you naturally associate with the upheaval. Once these symbols have all been collected, follow the writing instructions.

Instructions. Before you begin writing, spend several minutes looking at, feeling, and even smelling the various symbols. Let yourself experience some of the sensations and emotions of the past. (Warning: If you get too upset doing this, then stop and go to the store and get some ice cream instead.) After a few minutes, begin writing.

During the twenty minutes you write, explore your thoughts and feelings about this emotional upheaval. How has it affected you in the past, and how does it continue to influence you now? Briefly mention each of the symbols and explain why they are so powerful for you. You might tie this emotional experience to other aspects of your life — relationships, career, or family.

As always, write continuously and remember that this writing is for you and you alone. Also, remember the Flip-Out Rule: if you get too upset by your writing, simply stop.

Many people find this exercise extremely powerful. Often, the mere ability to verbalize one's fears and experiences can help reduce their sway. Similarly, linking emotional experiences to important symbols of the past can help clarify the meaning of a terrible experience.

If you found this exercise particularly valuable, try it again. The more times you do it, however, the more important it is to draw on other exercises in this book. That is, try to *use positive emotion words, construct a story, and change perspectives* each time you write.

Experimenting with a symbolic audience

The idea of a setting or context usually provokes thoughts of locations. Contexts, however, are also defined by the people inhabiting them. If you are in an empty classroom, the thought of a teacher is often inescapable. Your childhood home probably evokes memories of a host of other people. These "invisible" other people, then, become part of the context.

Once we begin thinking of people as part of a setting, we can't escape how the implied presence of others might affect our thoughts, emotions, and how we write. Throughout this book, most writing assignments have been explicit in getting you to write to yourself rather than to another person. But many scholars have debated whether doing so is even possible. While writing, you may have caught yourself thinking, "What will my friends (or spouse or child or enemy) think when they read this?" In reality, we change our writing depending on who we think the audience might be.

In this exercise, you will write to different symbolic audiences about an important personal experience. Although you will be asked to imagine that these other people will see your writing, don't show it to them. This writing exercise is for your eyes only.

General instructions. This exercise should take about twenty minutes. Your goal: write about the same general experience to four completely different audiences. Plan to write about five minutes to each audience. Your writing topic should be something emotionally important to you. It could be something that happened to you years ago or more recently. Ideally, write about something that involved another person close to you at the time. Whether they are alive today is not important. Once you begin writing, don't stop until five minutes are up. For each scenario, try to be as honest as possible.

Audience One: Authority figure. Imagine you must tell an authority figure in your life about this emotional experience. This authority figure must not be a part of the story. The person could be a judge, boss, FBI agent, parent, or teacher. It should be someone you have had a fairly formal relationship with or someone you respect and slightly fear. Imagine that your writing will be evaluated by this authority figure.

In your writing, tell the authority figure about this important emotional experience in your life. What were your thoughts and feelings then and now, and how has this experience affected your life since?

Audience Two: A close and compassionate friend. Write about the same experience but this time imagine you will show your writing to a close friend. This friend should be someone you deeply trust and who will accept you no matter what you say. Also, this friend should not be linked to the experience in any direct way. If you can't think of such a friend, invent one.

In your writing, tell your friend about this important emotional experience in your life. What were your thoughts and feelings then and now, and how has this experience affected your life since?

Audience Three : Another person involved in this experience. For this five-minute writing exercise, imagine that your writing will be evaluated by someone directly related to this experience. Ideally, choose someone with a very different perspective about what happened and its meaning.

In your writing, tell this person about this important emotional experience in your life. What were your thoughts and feelings then and now, and how has this experience affected your life since?

Audience Four: Yourself. For the final five-minute task, you should be the only audience. Now you are writing for yourself and no one else. To make the experience more powerful, consider looking at yourself in a mirror before you start writing. Imagine that you will destroy this writing sample as soon as you are finished.

In your writing, tell yourself about this important emotional experience in your life. What were your thoughts and feelings then and now, and how has this experience affected your life since?

Now that you have completed all four writing tasks, analyze how they differed. Did you feel different as you were writing them? Did some tasks feel more genuine than others? Did any one task give you a different perspective on your experience?

This kind of writing assignment can be effective in learning to appreciating the roles others play in our personal stories. You might benefit from writing to more than one imagined audience. If you find that your story changes a great deal from audience to audience, you probably don't have a good understanding of it just yet. As with the perspective-changing exercises, writing to different audiences can help give you a greater sense of detachment about the experience.

Playing with Writing Times

Some people work best in the early morning, and others do better late at night. When you write is a matter of personal preference. As noted earlier, the only recommendation about when you write is that you have free time after writing. That free time could be spent walking, driving, gardening, washing dishes, or similar activities. Watching TV is a bad idea — it naturally blocks our ability to self-reflect. After important writing sessions, it is essential that you have some time to continue thinking about your writing topic.

You may already have established your best times for writing. Nevertheless, it never hurts to shake up your schedule a bit. Experiment with some of the writing exercises in this book at different times of the day. Some possibilities include:

Early-morning writing. As soon as you wake up in the morning, begin writing. You can write in bed or in some other place in your home. Decide what your topic will be before you go to bed. Feel free to change the topic based on how you feel that morning. Also, draw on any dreams from the night before.

Lunchtime writing. Most of the exercises in this book take ten to twenty minutes. Even at work, you may find time for serious writing over your lunch break. Ideally, your writing should start as soon as your break begins. This will allow you some free time after writing to reflect. You can even do this task in place of eating a large lunch. So you can learn about yourself and lose weight at the same time!

Before-bedtime writing. At the end of a busy day, expressive writing can be a welcome escape. Many people fear that bedtime writing will give them nightmares. In fact, this does not happen with most people. If it does happen with you, however, then don't write just before bed. In one study with late night disclosure, researchers found that people who wrote before bedtime actually went to sleep more quickly and slept better than people who were not given the opportunity to disclose their thoughts and feelings.

Middle-of-the-night writing. I have spoken with a person who set his alarm clock to go off at 3:00 in the morning. He would silently get out of bed and write for twenty minutes. He swears by his technique. Try it if you want.

Talking into a tape recorder in bed. Go to bed with a tape recorder in your hand. Once the lights are out, simply talk about your thoughts and feelings into the microphone. This is recommended for people who don't have a sleeping partner, of course. In one experiment using this method, participants reported that it helped the quality of their sleep.

It never hurts to exercise your mind and to break out of your usual routines. Experiment with new times and places to write. Judge for yourself what works best and why.

10

Writing Creatively with Fiction, Poetry, Dance, and Art

The expressive writing techniques in this book encourage you to express yourself in words. Through writing, you can begin to construct meaningful stories of deeply personal experiences. Writing, of course, is not the only way to express yourself. Dancing, singing, painting, acting, and many other art forms can also help us get a grip on emotional upheavals.

In this chapter, you are encouraged to draw from your creative side. Let your emotional experiences in the past be expressed through other forms of writing or art. As you will see, each of these techniques relies on the power of words in some way. However, our brain's inventiveness can help us make better and more insightful stories.

Fiction Writing: Constructing Imaginary Stories

The more you write about emotional and personal topics, the more you can appreciate the fine line between expressive writing and creative writing. You can't help but wonder where personal narrative ends and fiction begins. Does writing fictionalized stories improve health as much as exploring your own experiences? Possibly. A fascinating study conducted in the mid-1990s by Melanie Greenberg and her colleagues had people write about traumas that had never happened to them. The participants wrote about the traumas as if they had really occurred in their own past. Amazingly, people writing about these imaginary traumas showed significant health improvements.

Before we discuss why writing imaginary stories might be good for your health, try the following twenty-minute writing exercise. The box below includes the basic information on four different traumas. Your task is to choose one of the traumas — ideally one that is *least* relevant to your life. Do not choose any trauma that has happened to you or a close friend.

Four Imaginary Traumatic Experiences

1. On returning home from work, you learn that your house of fifteen years has burned to the ground. All of your possessions — clothes, jewelry, pictures, and reminders of the past — are destroyed. The police arrest you on charges of arson, even though you aren't guilty. You are eventually freed. You have moved in with a cousin while you think about what to do.

2. You go to a restaurant with three fun-loving friends. After eating, the others talk you into running out the door without paying. The four of you jump into your car and begin to leave. The waitress runs out to flag you down. You accidentally hit her, which will put her in a wheelchair for the rest of her life. You get away and are never caught. You never see these friends again. You soon move to another town, but the memory of the event continues to haunt you.

3. You have been married for seven years in what you think has been a good marriage. You accidentally discover that your spouse has been involved in a love relationship with your best friend for over a year. You learn that all of your friends and family have suspected this the entire time. After you confront your spouse, your friend and spouse abandon you. It is now two years after your divorce and you are about to go out on your first date.

4. When you were ten, your mother remarried. She is happier than you have ever seen her. One night after drinking heavily, your stepfather

comes into your room and fondles you. He threatens that if you ever tell anyone, he will deny it. For the next five years, this happens a dozen more times. You never tell your mother. You think about this every day and wonder how it is influencing you now.

Writing Instructions

Choose one of the four scenarios listed above that is *least* relevant to your own life. Now imagine that this event happened to you. Really let go and try to feel the emotions and consider the thoughts you would currently have. Take at least ten minutes to relax deeply while thinking of this event. Create scenes in your mind and make them as vivid as possible. Finally, put yourself in the present and consider what it would be like for you now dealing with this trauma.

For the next twenty minutes, write about this trauma as if it really happened to you. Explore your very deepest emotions and thoughts about this event. How might it be related to other events in your life? How must this trauma have affected you when it happened? How does it affect you now? What meaning can you discern from this event?

After thinking deeply about this experience, begin writing. Write continuously for a minimum of twenty minutes.

When you have finished writing, analyze how it affected you. To what degree were you able to adopt this trauma as your own? Did you find it valuable or meaningful to write about it? One reason that writing about imaginary traumas may be helpful: all of us have experienced terrible events that involve loss, humiliation, secrecy, betrayal, and rage. Even though you may not have had your house destroyed, you know what it is like to feel alone or falsely accused of something. Writing about imaginary traumas can help us give meaning to confusing emotional experiences in our own lives.

If you found this exercise valuable, try it again using one of the other traumas. Or for that matter, pick a tragedy out of today's newspaper and write about it as if it happened to you. In addition to helping you come to terms with some of your own emotional issues, it should also make you more empathic about others' plights.

Experimenting with Poetry

Although there has been very little scientific research on the healing power of poetry, it is commonly used in psychotherapy. Intuitively, it seems that expressing emotions about powerful experiences through poetry should have positive health effects. Unlike straight prose writing, poetry often captures the contradictions of emotions and experiences.

Most people who enjoy expressive writing also appreciate poetry. For this next exercise, recall or find a favorite poem. As you think about or read a meaningful poem, fall into the emotion and cadence of it. If you don't have a poem handy, enjoy Robert Frost's well known "The Road Not Taken."

> *Two roads diverged in a yellow wood,*
> *And sorry I could not travel both*
> *And be one traveler, long I stood*
> *And looked down one as far as I could*
> *To where it bent in the undergrowth;*
>
> *Then took the other, as just as fair,*
> *And having perhaps the better claim,*
> *Because it was grassy and wanted wear;*
> *Though as for that, the passing there*

Had worn them really about the same,

And both that morning equally lay
In leaves no step had trodden black.
Oh, I kept the first for another day!
Yet knowing how way leads to way,
I doubted if I should ever come back.

I shall be telling this with a sigh
Somewhere ages and ages hence:
Two roads diverged in a wood, and I —
I took the one less traveled by,
And that has made all the difference.

Writing instructions. For this writing assignment, transform a personal experience of yours into poetry. It doesn't need to rhyme. It should be as free-form as you want. Turn off your mind's censor and touch an emotion, thought, or dream that is deep within you right now. Let the feelings crystallize into words. Let's dispense with the time limit — write as long as you want.

Nonverbal Expression and Words: Dance and Art

Are words necessary for healing to occur? If you could express a trauma through dance, music, or art, would you get the same benefits as you would through writing? This question has been tested with a group of college students using a form of dance therapy. The results suggest that nonverbal expression is powerful in making people feel better. Better yet, if they employed both bodily movement and writing, the healing effects were magnified. There is good reason to believe that translating emotional experiences into language can solidify long-term changes in thinking more efficiently than just using nonverbal expression.

In fact, most nonverbal therapies — art and dance therapy in particular — employ both nonverbal expression and language. Generally, the person is encouraged to first express an emotional upheaval through drawing or movement. When finished, the person is encouraged to talk about their artistic product. It may well be that the combination of both nonverbal expression together with writing (or talking) may be one of the most powerful healing strategies available. Unfortunately, this has not been tested in enough laboratories yet. In this section, two brief exercises are recommended — one involving dance and the other art. Try them and see if they are worthwhile.

Expressive Movement and Writing

For this exercise, find a place you can move around freely for at least ten minutes. It could be a living room with the tables moved out of the way. It could be a space outside, or even an empty garage or classroom. Ideally, find a place you can move around without others watching you (assuming you are at all self-conscious). If such a large, person-free space isn't realistic, try using your shower. Although this is referred to as a form of dance, no music is necessary.

For ten minutes, use movement to express your deepest thoughts and feelings about the issue or event that is most significant in your life. It may be a traumatic experience or one that has been very problematic or upsetting. It may be a current situation or conflict, or it can be something from the past still very much on your mind. The important thing is to express with your body's movement what you have never been able to say in words. What you do and how you do it is entirely up to you. There is no right or wrong way to move your feelings. It's your body, and only you know your experience and what you feel inside. Start with what makes sense to you. You can move on the floor, stand, or use the room in any way. You may move quickly or slowly, strongly or softly. You might use areas of your body that you normally don't consciously use expressively, like your spine, your feet, your face, your shoulders. The only requirement is to *keep moving* the whole time; even if you are expressing a stuck, tired, or rigid feeling, there is always a way to translate it into action.

After your ten minutes of movement, find a place to write for a minimum of another ten minutes. In your writing, explore your thoughts and feelings about your movement experience. What was going on in your mind and body? What were you expressing? What did your body tell you that you might not have been aware of? Use this time to try to understand both the emotional upheaval and your reaction to it. Once you begin writing, continue without stopping for at least ten minutes.

Many people find the expressive movement experience strangely powerful. You might find yourself analyzing what you did and why in the hours afterwards. Sometimes your movement may have great significance — other times it might not. If you find this form of expression useful, try it for several days in a row.

Artistic expression and writing

Just as expressive movement can help to draw out issues you may not have considered, other forms of artistic expression can do the same. Drawing, painting, sculpting, and other visual arts have long been known to express peoples' deepest thoughts and feelings. Although I believe that artistic expression is physically healthy, no studies have yet demonstrated it. Despite this, there are enough case studies for us to trust our instincts.

For the art-writing exercise, first draw, then write. You may or may not be able to draw even a straight line — that's not relevant here. You can, however, express yourself through drawing or even doodling.

For the next ten minutes, use blank paper — perhaps from a copier or printer — to express an emotionally important event, conflict, or feeling. Your drawing can be abstract, concrete, or seemingly random. The important thing is for you to really let go and express your very deepest emotions and thoughts by drawing. Don't judge yourself during the time you are drawing — just let your pencil or pen do the work. Once you begin, keep drawing without stopping. Use additional paper if you need to. The important thing is that you really free yourself and just *draw*.

After ten minutes, study your drawing. What was going through your mind as you were working? What were you feeling? Think about this experience for a couple of minutes. Now use expressive writing. Translate your drawing experience into words. Draw on your emotions and thoughts. Address issues about the emotional upheaval as well as the drawing experience.

This particular exercise relied on drawing. If you prefer, try other art forms. Many people like the sensuality of finger painting, the playfulness or dimensionality of clay, the vividness of acrylic or watercolors, or another artistic medium. For the purpose of this exercise, the drawing period was only ten minutes. You might want to devote an entire afternoon to expressing yourself about an important emotional experience. Indeed, you need not limit yourself to traditional art forms. People often express their deepest thoughts and feelings through woodwork, gardening, cooking, sewing, or playing with sand. Whatever you choose to do, consider writing about it afterwards. Putting emotional experiences into words provides an additional structure to an experience that can yield long-term benefits.

Art Prescription: Write to Heal

Here is an example of how writing and art may be combined. In a workshop called "Art Prescription: Write to Heal," cancer patients were asked to write about their experience of being diagnosed, then about their experience with cancer at any stage of treatment. They wrote for twenty minutes. Then they were given watercolor painting materials: brushes, paint, water, and a canvas. They were instructed to paint anything, any vision, any feeling that the writing seemed to provoke in them.

When the art was finished, participants told the story of their painting. One participant wrote that after the initial shock of being diagnosed, he began using a visualization technique. In it he imagined his body as an ocean and the cancer as a foreign material that could be cleaned out by roving cancer-eating fish. The fish were red with a line or touch of green. The cancer patient said the green and red represented life or the life force and actors in the immune system. In the lower third of the painting, he used dark brown colors, presenting a murky or muddy looking ocean bottom. In the middle third of the painting, colors lightened to include light green and yellow with wavy lines that suggested dark blue, pure water. In the topmost third, the dominant color was blue, with figures that suggested many swimming fish. In the top third, two ovals dominated. They were connected in the middle like a pair of goggles or glasses, perhaps suggesting a benign watchful presence.

Here is the painting. You can see a color version the website: ExpressiveWriting.org

PART III

Transform Your Health: Writing to Heal

To write about what is painful is to begin the work of healing.

— *Pat Schneider,* How the Light Gets In

Congratulations: You have arrived at Part III of this book, either because you finished reading the first two parts or because you decided to plunge right into the six-week program in writing for health.

Transform Your Health: Writing to Heal is a six-week program created by John Evans. Based on the first two parts of this book, this program is designed and organized as a progression of writing activities, each one building on the other. The writing sessions begin with expressive writing based on the original research described in Chapter 3. From this closely personal and private expressive writing, the exercises then progress from surviving a trauma to creating a legacy of resilience.

Each of the following chapters provides a writing exercise intended for one week of writing. The amount of time you spend writing will vary. Most writing assignments are designed to take twenty minutes, though some may take a little longer and require several short periods of writing each day for two or three days of the week. You may find it useful to set aside a specific day, time, and place to do the writing presented in these chapters.

The writing prompts should be completed in the order they are presented. Remember that you are in charge of setting your own schedule for writing. Be flexible in creating space for your writing. Taking a break from the writing — and the thinking and feelings it evokes — is important. You are encouraged to complete short surveys after each writing session to track your responses to the exercises. Examples from other writers provide comparisons you may find interesting. Your responses may differ greatly from what you read here, but please don't worry about that; this is not a competition.

Here is the weekly schedule described in Part III.

- Week One: Expressive Writing
- Week Two: Transactional Writing
- Week Three: Poetic Writing, Part One
- Week Four: Poetic Writing, Part Two
- Week Five: Affirmative Writing
- Week Six: Legacy Writing

Although a rich research base supports the expressive writing prompts in the first week's writing exercises (see Chapter 1), research regarding transactional, poetic, affirmative, and legacy writing is only in the beginning stages. Responses to post-writing surveys from over two hundred participants describe how participants perceived the effectiveness of the writing exercises and underscore the potential of further research. We urge you to be your own scientist and observe what you find when you try this approach to writing.

Let's get started.

11

Expressive Writing

Our own wounds can be vehicles for exploring our
essential nature, revealing the deepest textures of our
heart and soul, if only we will sit with them, open
ourselves to the pain ... Without holding back, without
blame.

Wayne Muller, Legacy of the Heart

Welcome to your first day of the six-week program, *Transform Your
Health: Writing to Heal.* Here you will find instructions for the
expressive writing experience also described in Chapter 3. If you already
did that writing, you may wish to skip ahead to Chapter 12. Or if you did
the writing in Chapter 3 some time ago, you may wish to try it again. To
help your planning, read these guidelines for the four days of expressive
writing sessions. Following the guidelines, you will find the expressive
writing prompts.

Time: Write for a minimum of twenty minutes per day for four
consecutive days.

Topic: What you choose to write about should be personal and
important to you.

Write continuously: Don't worry about punctuation, spelling, and
grammar. If you run out of things to say, draw a line or repeat what you
have already written. Keep pen on paper.

Write only for yourself: Plan to destroy or hide what you are writing. Do not turn this exercise into a letter. The exercise is for your eyes only. Letters can come later, if you wish.

The Flip-Out Rule: If you get into the writing and you feel that you cannot write about a certain event because it will push you over the edge, STOP writing!

What to expect: Some people feel a bit saddened or down after expressive writing, especially on the first day or two. Most people report that this kind of sadness is similar to hearing a sad story from a friend or watching a sad movie or television show. While sadness may linger, it usually lifts after an hour or so as you engage in other activities. Record how you feel using the post-writing survey. Give yourself some time after writing to reflect on what you have written. Be patient and compassionate with yourself.

Writing process: On the first and second day, allow yourself at least twenty minutes for writing. Be sure to also allow a few minutes after writing to relax and reflect on your writing. The topic remains essentially the same for both the first and second days. On the third day, you will shift your writing so that you are considering the topic from a different perspective or different point of view.

Write about how this event shaped your life and who you are. Explore especially those deep issues you may feel particularly vulnerable about. On the fourth day, you will stand back and think about the events, issues, thoughts, and feelings you disclosed. Really be honest with yourself about this upheaval, and do your best to wrap up your writing about this topic in a meaningful story that you can take with you into the future.

Day One Writing Instructions

Remember that this is the first of four days of writing. Today, your goal is to write your deepest thoughts and feelings about the trauma or emotional upheaval that has been influencing your life the most. In your writing, really let go and explore this event and how it has affected you. To start, it may be beneficial to simply write about the event itself, how you felt when it was occurring, and how you feel now.

As you write about this upheaval, you might begin to tie it to other parts of your life. For example, how is it related to your childhood and your relationships with your parents and close family? How is it connected to those people you have most loved, feared, or been angry with? How is this upheaval related to your current life — your friends and family, your work, and your place in life? And above all, how is this event related to who you have been in the past, who you would like to be in the future, and who you are now?

Remember to write continuously the entire twenty minutes. And never forget that this writing is for you and you alone.

At the conclusion of your twenty minutes of writing, read the section "Post-Writing Thoughts" and complete the post-writing questionnaire.

Post-Writing Thoughts, Day One

Congratulations! You have completed the first day of writing. Before setting aside your writing for the day, please answer the following questionnaire. Put a number between 0 and 10 by each question.

0	1	2	3	4	5	6	7	8	9	10
Not at all					Somewhat					A great deal

_____ A. To what degree did you express your deepest thoughts and feelings?

_____ B. To what degree do you currently feel sad or upset?

_____ C. To what degree do you currently feel happy?

_____ D. To what degree was today's writing valuable and meaningful for you?

E. Briefly describe how your writing went today so you may refer to this later.

For many people, the first day of writing is the most difficult. This kind of writing can bring up emotions and thoughts that you may not have been aware of. It may also have flowed more easily than you expected — especially if you wrote about something you have been keeping to yourself for a long time.

If your writing is something you don't want anyone to see, you can get rid of it now: destroy the paper, tear the pages out of your journal, delete the computer files, or erase the notes from your e-book. If keeping your writing for a while is not a problem, do that. It will allow you to go back at the end of the four days of writing and analyze what you wrote. You can always destroy the writing later.

Now, take some time for yourself. Until tomorrow.

Day Two Writing Instructions

Today is the second day of the four-day process. In your last writing session, you were asked to explore your thoughts and feelings about a trauma or emotional upheaval that has affected you deeply. In today's writing, your task is to *really* examine your very deepest emotions and thoughts. You can write about the same trauma or upheaval as yesterday's, or you can choose a different one.

The writing instructions today are similar to those for your last writing session. Today, try to link the trauma to other parts of your life. It is important to appreciate that a trauma or emotional upheaval can often influence every aspect of your life — your relationships with friends and family, how you and others view you, your work, and even how you think about your past. In today's writing, begin thinking how this upheaval is affecting your life in general. You might also write about how you may be responsible for some of the effects of the trauma.

As before, write continuously for the entire twenty minutes and open up your deepest thoughts and feelings. At the conclusion of your writing, complete the post-writing questionnaire.

Post-Writing Thoughts, Day Two

You have completed the second day of the four-day writing exercise. Before putting away your writing for the day, please complete the following questionnaire. Put a number between 0 and 10 by each question.

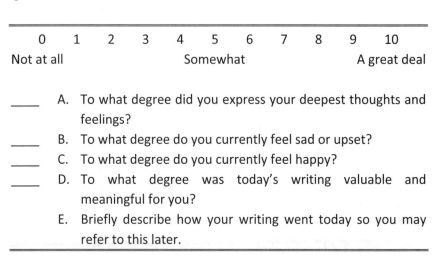

	0	1	2	3	4	5	6	7	8	9	10
Not at all					Somewhat					A great deal

_____ A. To what degree did you express your deepest thoughts and feelings?

_____ B. To what degree do you currently feel sad or upset?

_____ C. To what degree do you currently feel happy?

_____ D. To what degree was today's writing valuable and meaningful for you?

E. Briefly describe how your writing went today so you may refer to this later.

You now have two days of writing to compare. How did today's writing compare with your first day of writing? Did you notice that your topic was shifting? How about the way you were writing? Between now and your next writing session, think about what you have written. Are you starting to see things in a different light? How is writing affecting your emotions?

Now give yourself a little time to step back from your writing. Until tomorrow.

Day Three Writing Instructions

Congratulations! You have made it through two days of writing. After today, you will have only one more day of writing. Tomorrow, then, you will wrap up your story. Today, however, it is important for you to continue to explore your deepest thoughts and emotions about the topics you have been tackling so far.

On the surface, today's writing assignment is very similar to the earlier assignments. In your writing today, focus on the same topics you have been examining or shift your focus to another trauma or to another feature of the same trauma. Your primary goal, however, is to focus on your emotions and thoughts about those events that are affecting your life the most right now.

It is important that you don't repeat what you have already written in the past two exercises. Writing about the same general topic is fine, but you need to explore it from different perspectives and in different ways. As you write about this emotional upheaval, what are you feeling and thinking? How has this event shaped your life and who you are?

In today's writing, allow yourself to explore those deep issues about which you may be particularly vulnerable. As always, write continuously the entire twenty minutes.

Post-Writing Thoughts, Day 3

You have completed the next-to-last day of writing. Please complete the following questionnaire using a number between 0 and 10 by each question.

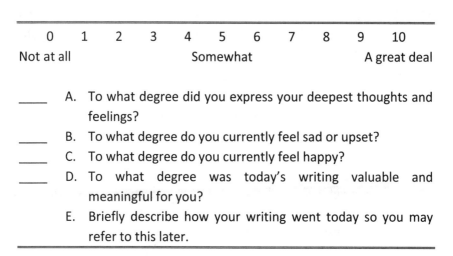

0	1	2	3	4	5	6	7	8	9	10
Not at all					Somewhat					A great deal

____ A. To what degree did you express your deepest thoughts and feelings?

____ B. To what degree do you currently feel sad or upset?

____ C. To what degree do you currently feel happy?

____ D. To what degree was today's writing valuable and meaningful for you?

E. Briefly describe how your writing went today so you may refer to this later.

In most studies, the third day of writing is highly significant. Here, people may uncover critical issues — issues they had been avoiding. Whereas the first two writing sessions can be like putting your toes in the water to see if it's too cold, by the third day some people are ready to jump completely in. A second group of people open up most on the first day. By the third day of writing they may be running out of steam. Both patterns are associated with improved health.

As with your last writing exercise, try to compare what you have written across the three sessions. What issues are surfacing as most important for you? Have you been surprised by any of your feelings while you were writing? Has the writing provoked any thoughts during the periods that you have been away from your writing?

Remember that tomorrow is that final day of the four-day writing exercise. The instructions for your last assignment will be much like today's. Since it will be the final day, however, think about how you will tie things up.

Now pamper yourself a bit. Until tomorrow.

writing surveys also show, on average, that writing was valuable and meaningful to the same degree the writers expressed their deepest feelings. In reflections about their expressive writing sessions, writers often discussed moving from negative language to more positive language. They describe how the traumatic event, while painful, has contributed something good to their lives or helped them become more compassionate toward themselves or others.

Many of the post-writing surveys reflect subtle realizations and expectations for welcoming the future. One participant wrote, "One sentence stood out for me, which ended with, 'and this is what I do not have settled in my heart' … while things seem less raw, there is an aspect of being unsettled about welcoming the new in the shadow of things past."

Not all post-writing surveys show dramatic movement. However, writers often report how their unexpected thoughts and feelings provided insights that they believe were discovered *because* they wrote.

One participant completed a post-writing survey and reflected this way.

Post-writing Survey — Expressive Writing Assignment

A. To what degree did you express your deepest thoughts and feelings: 10
B. To what degree do you currently feel sadness: 2
C. To what degree do you currently feel happy: 10
D. To what degree was today's writing valuable and meaningful to you: 10+++

Today I went to the next logical step in my writing, yet again, gaining some closure on the story of my upbringing. It has been the continuing saga of push and pull, weaving through angry feelings and a deep sadness for innocence lost. But today, out of a newfound understanding, my focus shifted from feeling like a victim to the motivations of my parent — their problems, their inability to become the persons they were intended to become. I ended up expressing thanks and gratitude and made peace with what they did give me because it made me the person I am.

Another participant completed the survey and reflected a bit differently.

Post-writing Survey — Expressive Writing Assignment
A. To what degree did you express your deepest thoughts and feelings: 8
B. To what degree do you currently feel sadness: 7
C. To what degree do you currently feel happy: 5
D. To what degree was today's writing valuable and meaningful to you: 9

I felt it in my body. I felt a gut-wrenching twinge as I wrote. I became aware of how little I recalled but also kept pushing the pen & I believe it didn't matter that I don't recall all the faces & details. It brought up the emotions & uncovered some faulty beliefs — but still honored my confusion, fault lines — It's like when coffins rise up in low-lying burial grounds — I came to a place of kindness to myself.

For another participant the writing became a means to see a stronger self.

Today I had a sense of resistance to the writing, as it seemed boring and distant to write about this again. But, then, the experience became a door through which I could see another event, more recent, very very fresh, that I do not yet know the full impact upon my life. What I recognized, though, was a similar threat to identity in a role and a relationship. Somehow, I feel stronger in the present.

Here is how a participant described all four days of writing.

I found working through the four assignments different to what I had expected. I think what I expected was sadness and regret and an "oh well, that's just the way it is" feeling.

*I began on the **first day**, sitting quietly and began to write, committed only to being as honest as I could be and to not censor my writing. I was writing about some events that took place about 20 years ago between the ages of about 18 and 22. I was shocked when the words I saw surfacing on my page were angry and wild. I hadn't expected so much anger, so aggressively expressed. On the **second day** of writing, my words changed and I saw sorrow surface from beneath the raw anger. A deep and anguished sorrow, which on the **third day** changed to sadness — sadness about the deep impact these events had had on my life, and the sense of loss I felt.*

*But the **fourth day** was interesting. So far my story had seemed angry, then sad, despair-filled, but when I began writing for the fourth day to bring the meaning together into my story, something shifted. I had images of the many wonderful things that I had experienced during my life too, the adventures, the many remarkable people I had met. I saw other things that were present — and greater — because of the quest and the seeking that these earlier events had inspired. Resilience, compassion, grace, humor, tenderness, mindfulness. I also saw how my way of responding to the events was deeply influenced by a cultural and social context that was conservative and patriarchal, but which was only one perspective. I was fortunate that this writing program came at the same time that I was completing a course in integrative health coaching and the two together had such a profound effect. A gratitude came over me and a new sense of purpose and groundedness. New hope to facilitate transformation in the lives of others, as so many have for me. A renewed sense of peace and confidence with myself. I am thankful for this new perspective.*

What is interesting in these responses and others like them is how the writers discover significance and meaning *as they write*. They are shaping their story at the point of utterance. Though they begin writing about an event in the past, they often end their writing in a way that shapes their present.

Looking at the language in the last example, we see how this writer moves from negative descriptive words such as *angry and wild, aggressively expressed, raw anger, deep and anguished sorrow, sadness* to more positive expressions such as *wonderful, remarkable, resilience, compassion, grace, humor, tenderness, mindfulness*. The writer concludes with "gratitude" and a "new sense of purpose and groundedness," "a renewed sense of peace," "confidence in myself," and "a new perspective."

Every writer's experience is unique.

When you are ready, look at your writing and your responses to what you wrote. Reading what others wrote and comparing that to what you wrote might provide insight. But keep in mind that your response is as unique as you are. As interesting as other responses are, yours are more important for your health. Notice your word choices. Are they negative, positive, or a mixture? What are the predominate pronouns? Is there movement in your story or does your story stay the same? Is there a change in your perspective or appreciation for another point of view? Have you described what things you have learned, lost, and gained as a result of this upheaval? Do you describe how these past events guide your thoughts and actions in the present and the future?

Before going to the next chapter and the next writing experience, take a break. Come back next week to begin your transactional writing experience. In the meantime, do something you love to do, and be gentle with yourself.

12

Transactional Writing

What is healing, but a shift in perspective?

Mark Doty, Heaven's Coast

Welcome to the second week of Transform Your Health: Write to Heal. Congratulations on finishing some very challenging assignments in expressive writing last week. Your work from last week should provide you with a good foundation for moving into this week's assignment: transactional writing.

Transactional writing is more formal than expressive writing, although the content may be just as personal. Transactional writing often occurs in professions or businesses; it offers an exchange of some value, meets the expectations of another, or completes an obligation. For the sake of writing-to-heal, consider that your transactional writing takes care of the business of your emotional life, whether new business or unfinished business, in order to express compassion, empathy, or gratitude.

Transactional writing's purpose is to complete an exchange of thoughts, beliefs, and feelings with someone else. For your transactional assignment, you may also consider some aspect of yourself as an audience. For instance, you may write a letter of compassion, empathy, or gratitude to your former self, to your future self, or to another aspect of yourself. Many participants do this, but most write to someone else: a friend, a family member, or a significant other. Sometimes participants write to an authority figure, sometimes to a stranger who played an important role in an experience.

Unsent or Sent. Don't worry about sending the letters you write as part of this transactional writing. In fact, it might be smart to *not* send the letters you write for this exercise. This exercise is ultimately for *your* mental health, not the intended recipient's. After finishing the exercise and taking a few days off, go back and look at your letters and consider if sending the letters would ultimately be beneficial for others. If your writings would not clearly benefit the person you wrote to, don't send them.

Observing Conventions. Unlike expressive writing, transactional writing observes some common conventions for letters, such as a greeting and a closing. In the act of writing any letter, the writer intentionally becomes conscious of another person, and this awareness greatly influences word choice, word order, and even the punctuation and sentence structure. So to a greater extent than expressive writing does, transactional writing observes language and style conventions like grammar, spelling, and punctuation, as much as the writer is able.

Shifting Perspective. Keep in mind: a guiding principle of transactional writing is to become conscious of another's perspective, and a defining characteristic of transactional writing is to communicate a message. However, don't make a concern for conventions your immediate or primary focus. Instead, concentrate on communicating your thoughts, feelings, beliefs, opinions, and judgments to another person. You are encouraged to write as many drafts of your letter as you wish, so don't worry about writing a perfect first draft.

Let's begin.

Your Transactional Writing Assignment

Read the three options below and choose the **one** that serves your purposes best. Or you may decide to combine elements from each option, but you need to write only one letter for this assignment. Of course, if you can't resist doing more, then go for it.

Choice #1 — The Compassionate Letter

Imagine if someone you love, your closest friend, your child, your partner, or your significant other had suffered the same trauma or traumas you wrote about in your expressive writing assignment.

In a compassionate and respectful way, write a letter with advice based on your experience. You might also do any or all of these:

- Write about what you wish you had known but learned later, and what you imagine they might learn from the event.
- Write about ways you are now growing and ways they may also grow.
- Write about any benefits from the crisis.
- Write about what your loved one might have learned about himself or herself from going through this difficulty.

In this letter to your loved one, use encouraging words of hope, comfort, and advice.

Choice #2 — The Empathetic Letter

Symbolically take your leave of the past and move forward by composing a letter to yourself or to someone else involved in the distressing event that you described in your previous expressive writing sessions. Try to understand why this person did, said, or acted the way they did. You aren't saying what happened is right, just, or fair. Instead, you're trying to understand and empathize. Start from the assumption that the person isn't a bad person; they just did something that hurt you or that you don't understand.

- What could they have been thinking?
- What could have happened to them in the past to make them do what they did?

- What might they have felt as they did it, and what might they have felt afterward?
- How do they feel now?

The goal of this letter is to understand how this person feels about the event.

Choice #3 — The Gratitude Letter

Write a letter to someone in your life to thank them for something they gave you, taught you, or have inspired in you. Get right to the point and don't apologize for not writing before now. Imagine how the recipient may feel when they read your letter. Describe your relationship with them and the context for this occasion. Describe the gift, the skill, or the inspiration you received from knowing them. In your letter, tell them:

- What their gift meant to you when you received it.
- How you felt about it then and now.
- How you have used this gift or the skill or the inspiration you received from them.
- How your life has been enriched by what you have received from them and by their presence in your life.

When you have made your choice about which letter to write, write the letter from start to finish. After you finish writing the first draft, go back and change or add anything you want. Rewrite as necessary until your letter is as good as you can make it. You may do this all in one day, or reflect on what you wrote and finish it the next day.

Remember that all writing for this session is confidential. You may share it if you choose, but there is no expectation for you to actually send this letter — or any of the letters, if you write more than one. If you send it, be sure it will help the recipient. Writing the letter, even without sending it, is all you need to do to help yourself.

When you are satisfied with the way you have done the transactional writing assignment, reflect on your experience and complete the post-writing survey below.

Post-Writing Survey — Transactional Writing Assignment

Congratulations! You have completed your transactional writing experience. Please complete the following questionnaire. Put a number between 0 and 10 from the scale below for each question.

0	1	2	3	4	5	6	7	8	9	10
Not at all					Somewhat					A great deal

_____ A. To what degree did you express your deepest thoughts and feelings?

_____ B. To what degree do you currently feel sad or upset?

_____ C. To what degree do you currently feel happy?

_____ D. To what degree was today's writing valuable and meaningful for you?

      E. Briefly describe how your writing went today so you may refer to this later.

Take a break before going to the next chapter and the next writing experience. You may wish to read how others reflected on their writing experience, or you may wish to relax and not think about writing right now. Both are perfectly fine! Come back next week to begin your poetic writing experience. In the meantime, do something you love to do, and be gentle with yourself.

Reflections on Transactional Writing

One participant wrote this in his response to the transactional writing session.

I wrote an empathic letter to my ex-wife. We were married for 32 years and we divorced 20 years ago. We meet a couple of times each year at my daughter's house, and we get along well. The divorce was very traumatic for me and difficult for her (though she requested it). My letter expresses my attempt to understand and sympathize with what I imagine were her feelings about our marriage. I have thought about her feelings many times but this was the first time I had written about them. The letter was difficult to write, and it left me with sad and regretful feelings. I certainly do not feel happy thinking about the marriage and divorce, but I feel a greater sense of calmness and closure after writing the letter. The experience has thus been very productive.

Another participant reflected this way.

I ended up writing two letters, although I had not initially planned to. I first wrote the Compassionate letter and found this to be deeply perspective-changing. Built upon the expressive writing assignment, it deepened and expanded the meaning and story I had chosen to move forward with. It also gave me further clarity on how I had become stuck in one viewpoint and in habitual thinking. That one viewpoint, being only one of the truths of the situation. It also made me so keenly aware of how I may, in many situations in life, judge others from a cultural perspective or social "norm," instead of seeking to "see" and know the person.

Although my recent [expressive] writing had not been directly related to my father, it did bring me to a deeper understanding of how my father's thinking had influenced me. In many ways, he has been a kind and dedicated father but his worldview of scarcity, fear, and perfectionism and his low self-esteem (often leading to narcissistic behavior) deeply affected our family.

In the second letter I was able to express my feelings about this, and see it in the context of his childhood and understand better where his worldview may have come from. I could also express sorrow that he was not able to address this with self-awareness as an adult, yet I ended up feeling a kind of acceptance and compassion.

Both were deeply meaningful experiences to write.

Here is what a participant said about a letter of gratitude he wrote to himself.

I wrote a letter of gratitude to that part of me that protected me from much of the effects of the significant trauma that I experienced as a child. I saw more clearly the amazing job that the "protector" part of me did, holding the pain, self-hatred, depression, and anxiety that came as a result of the trauma. I feel happy that my protector's job description has been changed & that he no longer has to bear this load that he never was truly meant to bear.

13

Poetic Writing

...our lives, any life, is worthy of poetry.
The experience of any human being
Is worthy of poetry.

— *Philip Levine*

Welcome to the third week of Transform Your Health: Write to Heal. Congratulations on finishing the assignments in transactional writing last week. Your work from the last two weeks should provide you with a good foundation for moving into this week's assignment: poetic writing.

Many of us get our definition of poetic writing from our school experiences, and we consider poetic writing something that requires a special gift — or at least an inclination for rhythm and rhyme. But let me assure you that no previous experience or affinity for writing poems is needed for these assignments.

To understand writing to heal, think of poetic writing more broadly than you might have learned in school. When writing for health and healing, poetic writing expresses the human condition using figurative language and narrative structures. Poetic writing then may include — but is not limited to — writing a poem or a narrative. The defining characteristics of poetic writing are metaphor, analogy, narrative structure, character, and imaginative descriptions of settings.

129

This week there will be two writing sessions, one on mindfulness and the other on mind/body connections. Each poetic writing session begins with a prewriting activity that encourages you through questions and discussion to focus on mindfulness or mind/body connections. Think of prewriting as a warm-up exercise for your writing muscles. Prewriting helps you discover what you have to say. After you finish prewriting, you will read a poem that was written by a participant in a Transform Your Health: Write to Heal six-week program. Think of this poem as a model for your own poem. Or think of the example poem as a scaffold. Its basic structure, including thematic words, line length, rhythm, metaphor, and repetition, will serve as a guide for your own poem. Here is a prewriting activity to get you started with writing a mindfulness poem.

Pre-writing for Mindfulness Poem

Take a deep breath or two or three. Breathe from the diaphragm. Slowly. Notice the rhythm of your breathing, how your body moves when you breathe deeply. Become aware of your thoughts as an observer who is not engaged in the thoughts. Just become aware. Be present without judgment, without trying to solve a problem or continue a dialogue.

Relax and let the words come naturally. Do not worry about form. Just let the words come. Turn off the inner critic. Be mindful of your words appearing across your screen as you press on the lettered keys, or be mindful of your pen or pencil moving across the page. Let the room fall away and just focus on your writing.

Write about your first thought as you lay in bed becoming awake this morning. Describe your awareness of the new day before you got out of bed. What was your primary thought? How did you sleep? Describe any dreams from last night. Describe any preoccupations that you may have had when you woke up. Describe your first glimpse of the day's weather as you got out of bed.

Describe how you felt as you got out of bed, physically and emotionally. Describe your morning preparations as you got ready for your day. Describe what you had to eat for breakfast. Write about your morning activities. What did you enjoy? Describe your pace or your morning rhythm. Describe your lunchtime. Did you eat alone? What did you eat? Drink? What was the best part? Write about your afternoon. Describe any music or radio program you listened to, or describe your preoccupations or any recurring thoughts through the day. What plans do you have for your evening or the time after you finish writing? How do you feel about these plans? How does this day fit in with the rest of your week?

Mindfulness Poem

Now read the poem below. A workshop participant used Jane Kenyon's poem "Otherwise" as scaffolding for her own poem (http://www.poemhunter.com/poem/otherwise/). In other words, she used Kenyon's metaphors, line length, thematic words, rhythms, and repetitions as a model to write her own poem about being mindful of her day. Read this original poem aloud twice, then write your own.

Otherwise
By a participant

I got out of bed,
Sheets silky, white cat purring,
It might have been otherwise.
I delighted

in a hot cup of tea.
It might have been otherwise.
I played with my children on
my bed. Laughter, tickling, joy.
All morning, I read, wrote and ran,
Some of my favorite things.
At noon I reveled in a hot shower, then
Went to a friend's house.
It might have been otherwise.
We ate dinner, Moroccan and delicious,
Drank wine, shared stories, laughed, ate more, drank more.
Friendship. It might have been otherwise.
I slept in a bed,
Hydrangeas outside my window,
My children's artwork on the walls and planned another
day,
Just like this one.
But one day, I know it will be otherwise.

After reading this poem aloud twice, try your hand at writing a poem about being mindful of your day. Use your prewriting for content if you wish. Use the poem's theme, rhythm, or repetitions as scaffolding for your own poem, or create your own theme, rhythm, or repetitions. If you like, feel free to start with the line: "I got out of bed…"

Post-Writing Survey — Mindfulness Assignment

Congratulations! You have completed your mindfulness writing experience. Please complete the following questionnaire. Put a number between 0 and 10 from the scale below for each question.

0	1	2	3	4	5	6	7	8	9	10
Not at all					Somewhat					A great deal

_____ A. To what degree did you express your deepest thoughts and feelings?

_____ B. To what degree do you currently feel sad or upset?

_____ C. To what degree do you currently feel happy?

_____ D. To what degree was today's writing valuable and meaningful for you?

       E. Briefly describe how your writing went today so you may refer to this later.

After you finish the mindfulness poem, take a break. It is probably best to wait until the next day to start on the mind/body connection poem.

Prewriting for a Mind/Body Connection Poem

After your prewriting instructions is a mind/body connection poem from a participant in a Transform Your Health: Write to Heal six-week program. Think of this poem as a model for your own poem. Or think of the example poem as a scaffold. The poem's basic structure, including thematic words, line length, rhythm, metaphor, and repetition, will guide your own poem. Here is a prewriting activity to get you started on a mind/body connection poem.

Take a few moments to think about how to describe your body and your relationship to it. How much of *you* is your body? Where are you if you are not your body? *What* are you if you are not your body? We know there is a relationship between our thoughts and our body because we have experienced a thought and then a response in our body to that thought, right? Think of blushing. Think of fingernails-on-a-chalkboard. Think goose bumps.

When you answer the above questions, just let the words come naturally. Don't worry if answers don't come quickly. Write whatever comes to mind in relation to the questions.

Now scan your body starting from head to toe and side to side. Be as fine-grained as you want, even down to the freckle, if you like. Don't worry about your form or make judgments. Just describe what you observe. Let the words come. Turn off the inner critic. Be mindful of the letters moving across your screen, or your pen or pencil moving across the page, and words filling up space. Be mindful of an old friend standing before you in your mind's eye. Let the room fall away and just focus on your writing. No one can see you or know what you are writing about.

Write about your first thought when you read "describe your body." Describe your awareness of yourself. What are your primary thoughts about your body? How do you like your whole self as you imagine yourself naked and standing before a mirror? Write about the parts you like and do not like, if that is the case.

Write about your legs, arms, feet, hands, hair, eyes, lips, belly, or whatever parts you would like to talk with. What would you like to say to your individual parts and to your body as a whole? Write about body parts you cannot see. Your organs. Your cells. Your bones. Your joints. Describe them all, if you like. What would you like to tell them, have them know, have them understand about you? Describe your brain and where the ability to write resides and is making decisions even as you type or write right now. What part of your mind is your brain, or is your mind part of your brain? Where is that place where you remember a dream or any dreams from last night or the night before that? Describe any preoccupations with a body part that you may have when you wake up in the morning. Describe your first glimpse of yourself in the mirror after you got out of bed today. Did you look better or worse than you felt? Describe the place where you believe that feeling resides. What story would your body tell about you?

Now write about a part of your body that you have had a challenging relationship with, or one that you have had a good relationship with after you learned to adjust your attitude about it. Maybe you didn't like this part and tried to change it. Maybe there is a part you do like and you have learned to show it off. Maybe you want to wear a shroud all summer long, or you yearn for the days that are so cold people have to wear hooded parkas or snowmobile suits. Maybe your eyes have always been your best feature and you know how to use them. Maybe there is another feature that you used to think was not so great, but now you use it to your advantage.

Mind/Body Connection Poem

After you have finished writing everything you can think of concerning your body, its various parts, and how they have affected who you are, read this poem by a workshop participant who used Lucille Clifton's poem *Homage to My Hips* (http://www.poetryfoundation.org/poem/179615) as scaffolding for a body part she'd had a challenge with but learned to appreciate. We are going to follow her example and pay homage to our body or some part of it.

Homage to My Nose
By a participant

This nose is a long nose, it's a family nose,
It needs freedom,
To be appreciated for what it is,
It doesn't like to be described
With disdain,
It adores the scents of food and flowers,
It smells beauty,
This nose is intuitive,
This nose is guiding,
I have known this nose to
Diagnose illness, to take joy in
The scent of a beautiful newborn baby.

Now try your hand at writing a poem about a part of your body. Use your prewriting for content if you wish. Use the poem's metaphors, thematic words, line length, rhythm, or repetitions as scaffolding for your own poem or create your own theme, rhythm, or repetitions.

Post-Writing Survey — Mind/Body Writing Assignment

Congratulations! You have completed your second poetic writing experience. Please complete the following questionnaire. Put a number between 0 and 10 from the scale below for each question.

0	1	2	3	4	5	6	7	8	9	10
Not at all					Somewhat					A great deal

____ A. To what degree did you express your deepest thoughts and feelings?

____ B. To what degree do you currently feel sad or upset?

____ C. To what degree do you currently feel happy?

____ D. To what degree was today's writing valuable and meaningful for you?

E. Briefly describe how your writing went today so you may refer to this later.

You may wish to read below how others reflected on their writing experience, or simply return to writing next week to begin your story telling experience. In the meantime, do something you love to do, and be gentle with yourself.

Reflections on Poetic Writing

The participant, whose poems we used as scaffolding, responded to the poetic writing sessions like this.

I enjoyed this assignment immensely, although I felt rather "clumsy." It reminded me of how much I love poetry. Words, expressed in a poem, move me and are powerful. They evoke all the senses...

...Otherwise, was a indeed a practice in mindfulness, for me. It brought me into the moment. It made me stand firmly in the ordinariness of my life — and I suddenly found myself filled with gratitude for the extraordinariness which I found there, just by looking closer, more intentionally.

The second part of the assignment made me aware of my mind-body connection. It made me realize that my thoughts and ideas are expressed in many ways, through my body. It made me realize how greatly I value a strong and healthy body, a resilient body. It made me want to take care of my body, thank her for all she does for me. I first wrote about my arms — "safe" writing for me. But then I went on to write about my nose — the more challenging relationship — and it actually filled me with a sense of humor (about how funny some of my thoughts of my nose have been!) and gratitude — that in the big scheme of things, what's a long nose anyway? I am just happy that it smells so many wonderful things and loves food!

Another participant responded like this.

I was really surprised! I am not poetic or read lots of poems other than the Psalms, but the structure or scaffolding allowed me not to worry about whether I could write a poem or not and immediately transported me to a lovely place where my thoughts could freely flow with the prompts serving as stepping stones. I was shocked actually that I really enjoyed this.

One participant described the experience this way.

Through these exercises I have affirmed the wonderful life that is mine as well as the fact that what makes me truly happy are life's simple pleasures. I also realized that I consciously feel my soul in my daily life on a regular basis. This takes practice.

And another participant wrote this about her experience.

This made me stop and appreciate what I have in my life. More than the other writing assignments, I saw the connection to mindfulness. In the other types of writing where the pen never stops it is difficult for me to feel the mindfulness because the flow of the pen feels a little bit like the flow of the thoughts in my head. This writing experience was more deliberate and made me focus on what was present now in my life.

Often I write along with participants and complete the assignments myself. Following the scaffolding of the Jane Kenyon's poem, I was able to reach a mindful place about my days. It reminded me that even the most ordinary of days are exquisite from a perspective of "Otherwise." I reached a place of gratitude for the ordinariness and routine of my days and praised their lack of drama — because I know sometimes, it is otherwise.

When I followed the scaffolding of the poem by Lucille Clifton, I found myself returning to my heart — not the romantic one and not the organ, but my abstract heart, that internal flywheel that keeps right on turning, keeps right on providing me with resilience and its touch of grace.

14

Story Telling

> We tell ourselves stories in order to live. ... We interpret
> what we see, select the most workable of multiple
> choices. We live entirely, especially if we are writers, by
> the imposition of a narrative line upon disparate
> images, by the "ideas" with which we have learned to
> freeze the shifting phantasmagoria which is our actual
> experience.
>
> — *Joan Didion,* The White Album

This week we move on to story telling In general, this includes any writing that is created with an imaginative approach. It is writing that appeals to our senses, uses metaphorical expression, and uses the ideas discussed in Chapter 7: a description of the setting, a sense of the main characters, a clear description of the event or upheaval, the immediate and long-term consequences, and the meaning of the story. Story telling can be fiction, personal essay, or creative nonfiction.

This week's assignment has several steps. Step one is reading creative nonfiction. Step two is writing a response to it. Step three is writing your own piece of creative nonfiction. Directions are provided for each step.

When you are finished with all three parts of this assignment, it may interest you to read how two participants completed the assignment and responded to each other's writing.

Step One: Reading "Salvation"

Read the following piece of creative nonfiction, "Salvation" by Langston Hughes. You may find that this piece reveals many insights into family dynamics, especially ones that surround a family's religious beliefs and a young person's unsuccessful rite of passage. But we're using Hughes's writing a bit more broadly than that. The topics for your writing in response to Hughes are not limited to religion or rites of passage. As you read, pay attention to the kind of words Hughes uses, especially his use of metaphor and the contrast between concrete and literal language.

Salvation

Langston Hughes

I was saved from sin when I was going on thirteen. But not really saved. It happened like this. There was a big revival at my Auntie Reed's church. Every night for weeks there had been much preaching, singing, praying, and shouting, and some very hardened sinners had been brought to Christ, and the membership of the church had grown by leaps and bounds. Then just before the revival ended, they held a special meeting for children, "to bring the young lambs to the fold." My aunt spoke of it for days ahead. That night I was escorted to the front row and placed on the mourners' bench with all the other young sinners, who had not yet been brought to Jesus.

My aunt told me that when you were saved you saw a light, and something happened to you inside! And Jesus came into your life! And God was with you from then on! She said you could see and hear and feel Jesus in your soul. I believed her. I had heard a great many old people say the same thing and it seemed to me they ought to know. So I sat there calmly in the hot, crowded church, waiting for Jesus to come to me.

The preacher preached a wonderful rhythmical sermon, all moans and shouts and lonely cries and dire pictures of hell, and then he sang a song about the ninety and nine safe in the fold, but one little lamb was left out in the cold. Then he said: "Won't you come? Won't you come to Jesus? Young lambs, won't you come?" And he held out his arms to all us young sinners there on the mourners' bench. And the little girls cried. And some of them jumped up and went to Jesus right away. But most of us just sat there.

A great many old people came and knelt around us and prayed, old women with jet-black faces and braided hair, old men with work-gnarled hands. And the church sang a song about the lower lights are burning, some poor sinners to be saved. And the whole building rocked with prayer and song.

Still I kept waiting to *see* Jesus.

Finally all the young people had gone to the altar and were saved, but one boy and me. He was a rounder's son named Westley. Westley and I were surrounded by sisters and deacons praying. It was very hot in the church, and getting late now. Finally Westley said to me in a whisper: "God damn! I'm tired o' sitting here. Let's get up and be saved." So he got up and was saved.

Then I was left all alone on the mourners' bench. My aunt came and knelt at my knees and cried, while prayers and song swirled all around me in the little church. The whole congregation prayed for me alone, in a mighty wail of moans and voices. And I kept waiting serenely for Jesus, waiting, waiting — but he didn't come. I wanted to see him, but nothing happened to me. Nothing! I wanted something to happen to me, but nothing happened.

I heard the songs and the minister saying: "Why don't you come? My dear child, why don't you come to Jesus? Jesus is waiting for you. He wants you. Why don't you come? Sister Reed, what is this child's name?"

"Langston," my aunt sobbed.

"Langston, why don't you come? Why don't you come and be saved? Oh, Lamb of God! Why don't you come?"

Now it was really getting late. I began to be ashamed of myself, holding everything up so long. I began to wonder what God thought about Westley, who certainly hadn't seen Jesus either, but who was now sitting proudly on the platform, swinging his knickerbockered legs and grinning down at me, surrounded by deacons and old women on their knees praying. God had not struck Westley dead for taking his name in vain or for lying in the temple. So I decided that maybe to save further trouble, I'd better lie, too, and say that Jesus had come, and get up and be saved.

So I got up.

Suddenly the whole room broke into a sea of shouting, as they saw me rise. Waves of rejoicing swept the place. Women leaped in the air. My aunt threw her arms around me. The minister took me by the hand and led me to the platform.

When things quieted down, in a hushed silence, punctuated by a few ecstatic "Amens," all the new young lambs were blessed in the name of God. Then joyous singing filled the room.

That night, for the first time in my life but one for I was a big boy twelve years old — I cried. I cried, in bed alone, and couldn't stop. I buried my head under the quilts, but my aunt heard me. She woke up and told my uncle I was crying because the Holy Ghost had come into my life, and because I had seen Jesus. But I was really crying because I couldn't bear to tell her that I had lied, that I had deceived everybody in the church, that I hadn't seen Jesus, and that now I didn't believe there was a Jesus anymore, since he didn't come to help me.

Step Two: Preparing to write about "Salvation" and your own experiences.

Consider these questions to help guide your reflection. What is happening as the primary scene unfolds? What does Hughes suggest when he writes: "I was saved from sin when I was going on thirteen. But not really saved." What is the source of confusion for young Langston? Why did he hesitate to join the others at the altar? What are the primary figures of speech that move between figurative language and literal language? How might your prior knowledge or previous experience explain Langston's dilemma? Write about what you believe is happening in "Salvation" and explain how you think Hughes may have incorporated his youthful church experience into his adult life. What, if anything, in Langston's experience resonates with your own experience?

If you have trouble getting started, skip ahead in the chapter to see what others wrote in response to these questions.

Step Three: Create a short creative nonfiction piece

Immediately after finishing Step Two — or the next day, whichever feels better — write a story of your own of about 300-500 words. In your writing, tell the story of a personal experience you had where you were able or unable, willing or unwilling to complete a family rite of passage or fulfill family expectations. Bring your story up-to-date by concluding with what you think about this now and how you incorporate this story into the fabric of your identity and your life now.

Post-Writing Survey — Story Telling Assignment

Congratulations, you have completed your story telling experience. Please complete the following questionnaire. Put a number between 0 and 10 from the scale below for each question.

0	1	2	3	4	5	6	7	8	9	10
Not at all					Somewhat					A great deal

_____ A. To what degree did you express your deepest thoughts and feelings?

_____ B. To what degree do you currently feel sad or upset?

_____ C. To what degree do you currently feel happy?

_____ D. To what degree was today's writing valuable and meaningful for you?

E. Briefly describe how your writing went today so you may refer to this later.

Examples of Nonfiction Writing and Responses

The examples offered here are different from those in other chapters because they are taken from an online version of Transform Your Health: Write to Heal offered in September 2012 through the International Association of Journal Writers. In the other chapters, I said you could read the examples if you wanted to. In this chapter, I *encourage* you to read them. It's okay if you don't, but there are some profound insights to be found here.

In the online version, participants did the same writing activities as they would in a face-to-face workshop, but instead they used Google Groups to read assignments, view others' responses to assignments, and post responses to others. There were twelve participants in this online workshop.

You will notice the writing is in a slightly different form than the writing in previous chapters. Instead of sharing only what participants wrote in post-writing surveys, I'm including fuller responses from two participants. Instead of reflections about their writing process, here is their actual writing in response to this assignment, my comments about their writing, and also comments from another workshop participant. Taking this slightly different approach may illustrate the dynamic quality of these writings and response patterns and the potential for rich engagement and exchange among participants in an online workshop.

Here is how a participant who wished to be known as Irish Rose responded to Hughes's creative nonfiction.

When Hughes writes he was saved from sin but not really saved he means he was aware he was not being true to himself. He hesitated joining the others at the altar because he was waiting for Jesus to appear to him or see a light, it didn't happen. This caused him deep grief. He, like many children, trusted the adults in the church.

Hughes was scared he was the one lost sheep because he believed his salivation was not true. This made him sad because no one wants to go to hell, especially a child. This caused him to be fearful but he was earnest and was waiting for a sign from Jesus.

The people in the church were caught up in an emotional high that bordered on insanity but Hughes being a child wanted to please those around him to be accepted and get the service over with since it was late and hot.

Hughes finally went to the altar, and cried that night in bed because it bothered him to lie. He came to the conclusion not to believe in Jesus since he did not come to help him.

I wouldn't doubt when Hughes became an adult he never allowed himself or his children to be subjected to radical religious beliefs. He would want to protect his children and himself from the guilt/shame they indoctrinate.

I would have a difficult time thinking Hughes ever believed in Jesus again. I think because of this experience he learned to be true to himself. I felt empathy for Hughes while reading the story. — Irish Rose

Here is what Irish Rose wrote as her response to Step Three.

Rescue

My mother had four children within five years, I was the youngest and the least wanted. That in fact my mother told me daily. By the time I was born she was very angry with her marriage and her life in general.

After my parents divorced, we relocated. My sister had to share a room with me for the first time. She always had her own room, and she was not happy with this arrangement. She was the oldest, two brothers were in the middle. The bedroom we were assigned was the largest room in the house with a small walk-in closet on each side. The bed was placed under the windows in the center of the room. My sister drew an invisible line down the center of the room, saying: "Don't ever cross over on my side of the room, or the bed, or else." She was five years older than I, a stocky girl, while I appeared thin and fragile.

My sister picked the closet on the left that had linoleum on the floor and wallpapered walls. My closet, on the right left much to be desired but I didn't complain. It had wide unpainted hardwood boards with large gaps between on the floor. The plaster was falling off and many slats showed through holes in the ceiling and walls. The ceiling slanted with the roofline so I could only stand up in the doorway, otherwise I had to bend over so I wouldn't hit my head.

The door to the bedroom was on the south wall in the middle of the room and the bed was under the windows opposite the door so keeping on my side was no problem. The thing I enjoyed about this arrangement was the light was attached to the wall on my side of the room. I spent many contented hours sitting on the floor, under the light, reading.

The problem was many times in the middle of the night while I was sleeping soundly, my sister would hit me in the face with her fist, cause a bloody nose, black eye, kick me in the stomach or rake my flesh open with her fingernails. I would run to the bathroom to wash my wounds. Then she would make me change the sheets before I could come back to bed, and warn me if it should happen again, getting too close to her side of the bed, I wouldn't be so lucky the next time.

After a few years of this punishment, for moving in bed, I suffered from insomnia and my grades were falling at school. I was so sleepy the teacher became blurry, and I could not concentrate. I became quiet, withdrawn, fearful of going to bed, and taught myself to freeze in position, clutching the binding of the mattress edge.

Because everyone loved my sister I didn't feel there was anyone I could talk to. She was the first grandchild, born on my grandfather's birthday, and the beauty queen of the family. She told lies and turned most of my aunts, uncles, grandparents and cousins against me. She called me "Witch" most of the time.

I had a cousin who was seven years older than I. He was kind and protective. He loved children. I thought it might be safe to talk to him because he took time with me, teaching me to shoot, teaching me the names of trees and wildflowers. He even helped me pull weeds in the garden. Finally, one day when we were looking for four leaf clovers in the field by the house I told him [about how I slept]. His first expression looked indignant, but, then he said, "Well, let's go see how big your closet is." Together, we moved the heavy steel rollaway bed from the front porch upstairs into my closet. We swept the cobwebs out and found an old sheet. He said, "You should be safe here." Now, the bed would not go flat, as the walls were too narrow, so I had to sleep in a sitting position. From that time on, until my sister married, I slept in a tiny, airless, windowless closet where at times fragments of plaster fell on me.

In my family's eyes my sister could do no wrong, so I kept quiet. My family swept unpleasant things under the rug, ignored them, or keep them a secret entirely. To my knowledge, either no one knew I slept in the closet, or they didn't care. But, I was safe at last and am eternally grateful to my cousin.

This experience taught me to be protective, sympathetic, and gentle with children. It caused me to be more comfortable sleeping alone. I learned I don't deserve to be mistreated and now take a stand against unfair deeds and bullies.

I have learned I was too forgiving, was searching for love and acceptance so I tried to please others and allowed them to mistreat me. I have learned it is acceptable to dislike some people. I can forgive them, or not, that is my choice, and it is all right.

I am not comfortable in the limelight but enjoy bringing others happiness, privately. There are few photos of me as a child because my sister thrived on attention. She lied, caused trouble, complained, and was a drama queen. She was loud, abrasive, nagging, cruel, and had a sob story to tell anyone who would listen.

Once, during one of Dad's visits I was sitting on the stairs while my sister talked to him for the entire duration of his time. Later, he took me aside and said, "Don't think I don't love you as much, but the squeaky wheel gets the grease." It was years before I understood what he meant.

Now, I embrace each day and enjoy God's creations. Every day brings joy and gratefulness for the beauty and goodness around me. I find peace in watching a leaf fall gently and silently to the ground, in music, art, yoga, travel, reading, and writing. I am delighted to be alive, to see, to hear, to love, and work. I am grateful for the love and friendship my daughter and I share and for my two precious grandchildren.

I find joy in volunteering, helping veterans, the elderly, visiting the home bound, and just recently reuniting a son with his biological father whom he had never met and had many genealogist searching for, for 25 years. This young man now has uncles, aunts, cousins, and a dad in Oklahoma. He is as overjoyed as his new found family. I have found fulfillment in doing small deeds to help others.

I am true to myself, have found peace because I learned that all of the light I will ever need is within me and my goal is to leave positive and loving memories behind. — Irish Rose

In responding to Irish, I wrote.

Dear Irish,

I wonder if you would care to share how it was for you to write about your bedroom in a closet? What did you feel as you wrote about it? How did it feel after you wrote it?

John

Irish responds to me.

Dear John,

Writing "Rescue" was emotionally exhausting and brought back more memories as I typed. I felt sad thinking of the child who was only trying to survive. Being in my closet made me feel safe but very alone and sad. My cousin turned out to be my protector for the rest of his life. He kept my secrets, never caused me any grief and from that time on spent more time at our house. The closet was never again mentioned for the rest of his life.

He told me he was the "Black Sheep" of his family, never felt he belonged, and was never favored either, and in the end we would both be better off. He always had a positive attitude and encouraged me. He is my childhood hero. He is the only one who ever saw me cry, and the only one who ever consoled me. I realized while writing that I suffered from depression during most of my childhood and learned from an early age to hide my real feelings.

After writing "Rescue" I felt a sense of relief, of letting go entirely. Actually I had not thought of the incident for many years but reading

"Salvation" ignited many childhood memories and scars. Your words, "Sometimes we have to make family out of those who are able to love us instead of those who are supposed to love us." brought me more healing than words could express, I thank you.

All good wishes,

Irish Rose

Here is a response to Irish from Seddon T., another participant in online Transform Your Health: Write to Heal.

Dear Irish,

Thanks for your response to my poem. I know that we all have scars and it means a lot that the poem helped you. I know that I am sometimes at odds with my body and it helped to rewrite the story as a past that I am moving forward from.

I am also touched by your honest writing about your family event in "Rescue." While I did not have the same event with a sister or sharing a room, I still understood what it felt like to not be believed or blamed for stirring things up. I was the oldest with two younger brothers. My brothers were expected to fight and be somewhat aggressive but if I did similar things I was told that I was being "angry." In other cases, when I was bullied at school, my brothers (who were more popular) would roll their eyes and say that I was being dramatic. In recent years, my mom has begun to acknowledge the inequities that occurred. But it is extremely painful to be somehow invisible in your own family. I am impressed that you took such gained such strength and empathy from a difficult situation.

I love the fact that you are "true to yourself"! Seddon T.

Irish writes back to Seddon T. in this way.

Thank you Seddon for your response to "Rescue." I must admit it was many years before I learned to be "true to myself." Life is interesting and this class has helped me open up. Actually, I did everything I could to win my sister's love and approval up until the past few years. She always took advantage of me and caused me grief until I realized I had no respect for her and let her go. Now, I am glad to be free of the drama and realized I have many sisters [friends], who respect me and encourage me.

Your encouragement has been refreshing, I appreciate that. Your poem was such an inspiration to me, I thank you. All my best, Irish Rose

Seddon T. explains how she approached her creative nonfiction assignment in response to "Salvation."

For my creative nonfiction writing, I chose to write about a situation in which I felt extremely judged by my parents when I was a late teenager and early in college. Suffice it to say, the conversation that I had with them left me wounded. I have recently discussed it with my mom. She took some time to reflect on it and apologized that she and my dad had handled the situation poorly and left me feeling like I was an embarrassment.

I am still not comfortable sharing the contents of the conversation but I can say that my parents left me with a feeling of shame. I was also disappointed in them because I had hoped that we could talk as adults during that time period.

In beginning to write this piece, I wrote out and picked from a number of scenarios in which I was confronted by family expectations. In some cases, I went along with my family's expectations; in others not. When I pinpointed the deeper, more difficult situations for me to write about, I felt somewhat nauseous remembering the past and how I was made to feel. The times when I felt worst were also the times when I didn't stand firmly on what I believed. I thought even more about how brave Langston Hughes was to write about his "Salvation" because he had to expose his innermost thoughts at the time and reveal (perhaps to those same family members) that he had to lie to make them feel better.

This was not an easy piece to write — in part because I chose a deep wound. But I realized in writing this, how important it is to be true to what I believe whether it is what my family or others want to hear. We can be haunted by the ghosts of things that we did not say or situations that we did not confront.

In terms of my own development, I have learned to listen carefully to others and try to understand what they really mean. I have also learned that sometimes it is enough to sit quietly with someone in a tough situation and not judge them when times are difficult.

Irish Rose responds to Seddon T.

You say we are haunted by the ghost of things we do not say or situations we did not confront. So many times the outcome might have been different if our response would have been different. If people would be willing to be humble and admit their wrongdoings the world would be such a better place. It begins in each of us, to learn and to teach others that it is not weakness but strength and it could go a long way in reconciliation of many relationships. It is inexcusable when parents cause their children to feel shame and it nauseates me also. It is not a loving parent who does that. I love these words of wisdom:

"When we honestly ask ourselves which person in our lives means the most to us, we often find that it is those who, instead of giving advice, solutions, or cures, have chosen rather to share our pain and touch our wounds with a warm and tender hand. The friend who can be silent with us in a moment of despair or confusion, who can stay with us in an hour of grief and bereavement, who can tolerate not knowing, not curing, not healing and face with us the reality of our powerlessness, that is a friend who cares."

An embarrassment? That is very unkind after apologizing for the way they handled it. Parents make mistakes, they are not perfect and should be willing to own up to their mistakes, we would have more respect for them in the end. I was naive and used to think there was a resolution to every problem, but I have learned there is not always a resolution and we must let it go and embrace the present moment, and find our own peace within.

Much of what you have written cuts me deeply, I wish you all my best through writing to heal.

Thank you for sharing. Kind regards, Irish Rose

Here is what I wrote to Seddon T.

Dear Seddon T.,

Thanks for sharing your reflection about writing your piece of creative nonfiction.

If you are not familiar with her work, you may find Brené Brown's TED talk on shame interesting: http://www.youtube.com/watch?v=psN1DORYYV0

You will know best if and when you wish to share your story with others, but it is not required for your work in this course.

Best wishes, John

And Seddon T. answers me.

Hi John —

WOW — that was an amazing TED talk on shame. I had tears running down my face the first time watching it. The second time through I could really listen closely.

I really identified with how Brené Brown distinguished shame and guilt: Guilt is "I'm sorry I made a mistake." Shame is "I'm sorry I AM a mistake."

I know that feeling of "being a mistake" too well unfortunately. However, identifying the shame that I have felt sounds like the first step towards healing from it. I am interested in hearing and reading more about Brené Brown's work on shame and plan to follow up with it.

Do you think that sharing my story would help put some of those feelings of shame behind me? I ask because the more that I think about my discomfort in sharing my creative nonfiction — the more that I realize that part of my hesitation with sharing was based around shame that was internalized. That somehow I would be judged and people would not see me the same way (even in this small group). I feel a lot of love and warmth from everyone (especially Irish's comments on my response) and see the deep wounds in those brave enough to share their own version of Langston's "Salvation."

Thanks for organizing this class and your support throughout this journey together. — Seddon T.

A few days later, Seddon T. decides to share her creative nonfiction.

Hi John —

I thought I'd share my creative nonfiction piece with you and others in case it does help relieve feelings of shame and help with me moving forward. You can comment or not — I am hopeful that this act of making myself a little more vulnerable and not keeping the story an ongoing secret might help me deal with its repercussions and feelings of shame that I was left with.

Thank you for your kindness in reading and discussing our stories. — Seddon T.

Seddon's Secret

At the end of my sophomore year of at college, I was home for the summer and riding along with my mother in the family mini-van returning from a shopping trip. My parents had emphasized an honest, open discussion of ideas and adult situations that I might encounter. Up until then, my parents seemed complimented that I was forthright with them and they promised that if I should ever need a ride home that I could call them without repercussion.

While driving, my mother casually mentioned that I should get my first gynecological examination soon and perhaps talk to the doctor about birth control. I swallowed, wondering if I could stop this conversation from happening. But I had always promised myself that if asked I would be honest and answer any questions asked of me. So... I cleared my throat and answered that I had already had my first gynecological exam at college and was already on the pill. The irony of this statement was that I had several friends at school that thought it was unusual that I had not already had a gynecological exam as a freshman (even though I was still a virgin at that point) and encouraged me to go to the doctor as a wise health choice. I had taken their recommendation and had gone on the pill to help control my extremely heavy and painful periods.

My mother simply responded, "Oh." The whole rest of the car ride was silent. We did not talk about why I had made the choice to go ahead and take care of my feminine needs or whether I was sexually active. I had only recently become sexually active and quite honestly the birth control was not intended for that purpose.

When we got home, she said that we would talk to my father about this and that I could wait in my room till he got home from work. He got home early and the three of us sat down. They never asked me any questions to start things off and immediately my father started telling me how disappointed he was in me. He said that they had expected more from me. I was quite surprised that I was receiving a lecture given that I had remained a virgin until quite recently and felt that I had been responsible in handling my decisions. My mother said very little during this encounter.

I was shocked at the lecture and the words that were used. I felt like they were calling me a slut and vowed never to open up emotionally again about what was really going on deep inside me. What they didn't know and didn't ask about was that a year prior, I had sex for the first time in what was quite close to a date rape situation. They still don't know about that and assumed that I had chosen recently to have sex with my boyfriend at that time. I remember that I closed down and that was the last time that I opened up to them about something deep and personal for years.

To this day, I still don't discuss sex or boyfriends in front of them even though it's been another 19 years. Recently, I finally talked to my mom about the way that they handled "the talk." She had blocked a large part of it out and was upset to realize that she had left me feeling like they thought I was a dirty slut.

I still find it difficult to consider dating around them, and it is strange to live close to them now. After college, I lived about 12 hours away from home for 18 years of my life in Boston and Chicago and found it was easier because I could keep my "home" and "family" life separate.

I am still unmarried for a number of reasons but I wish the subtle looks of disapproval that I get when I mention dating or going to a party with friends would go away. At 38, you would think I had earned the right to be treated as an adult, not a "dirty" teenager.

15

Affirmative Writing

> Your work is to discover your work, and then with all
> your heart to give yourself to it.
>
> — *Gautama Siddhartha*

You have now completed four weeks of our six-week Transform Your Health: Write to Heal program. You may feel that you have done some very heavy lifting in the first four weeks. I am reminded that, as Natalie Goldberg says in *Old Friend from Faraway*, "Writing is an athletic activity.... The muscles of writing are not so visible, but they are just as powerful: determination, attention, curiosity, a passionate heart."

I am also reminded that the kinds of writing you have done and are doing take time to have their full effects and benefits. One day in the next few weeks, you will realize that something that had been worrisome is just... not there. You will not realize that the weight is lifted from you until it floats into consciousness, and then you may say, "Oh, that old thing again. Isn't it interesting how I'm thinking of it now in more mindful, nonjudgmental awareness?" Thinking of your future like this is a good way to begin our week of affirmative writing.

Like expressive and poetic writing, affirmative writing can be personal and emotional writing. However, in addition to expressing our emotions, affirmative language often provides life-course corrections. Affirmative writing allows us to re-perceive things through imaginative

158

selection and arrangement of words that describe our goals, aspirations, and intentions in positive language.

In affirmative writing, we pay attention to the present and look forward to the future by writing about our strengths in body, mind, and spirit. Affirmative writing describes our desired outcomes or feelings as if they are already in our possession. With affirmative writing, we express realistically achievable goals or growth in positive language using first-person, present-tense language. ("I am…") For some, the term affirmative writing means "writing it forward" because we're writing about qualities we wish to affirm are available to us in the future. In this way, we write to support a flourishing life filled with goodness, generativity, growth, and resilience.

Affirmation Writing Exercise

In this exercise, we consider how we strive for self-actualization. What does self-actualization mean for you? What, if anything, do you wish you could change about yourself, your whole life, or physical, emotional, or spiritual aspects of your life? Consider your current state and your desired outcomes for your physical, emotional, and spiritual dimensions. Imagine yourself six months from today. Perhaps you want to look at a calendar and mark that day in your electronic or paper journal.

Looking into the future, write a descriptive paragraph about yourself. To guide your writing, consider: What do you look like at your personal best six months from now? What is the image that comes to your mind? Describe your face and how it reflects your state of mind. Describe your prevailing mood. How is that reflected in your self-talk? Describe your diet. Your sleep. Your regular or new habits. How do you spend your time? Describe your interactions with others. Your relationships. Your work. Write as much as you like. Take as much time as you need. Write as much detail as you need. Write about your future self in the first person, present tense. Start with the words "I am."

For example, you may start like this:

I am a vigorous, energetic person with a calm demeanor. My face, though older, is calm with a quality about it. I'm like people of a certain age whose eyes may have a hint of humor or quiet amazement. People tell me I look calm and peaceful. I feel a quiet strength in my body and balance in my life. My diet is filled with good but simple, natural ingredients, a glass of wine now and then. I exercise regularly, practice mindfulness, and write regularly. I enjoy my family and friends. I am grateful that I am more mindful of life's wonders every day…

Post-writing Survey — Affirmative Writing Assignment

Congratulations! You have completed your affirmative writing experience. Please complete the following questionnaire in your journal. Put a number between 0 and 10 from the scale for each question.

	0	1	2	3	4	5	6	7	8	9	10
Not at all					Somewhat						A great deal

_____ A. To what degree did you express your deepest thoughts and feelings?

_____ B. To what degree do you currently feel sad or upset?

_____ C. To what degree do you currently feel happy?

_____ D. To what degree was today's writing valuable and meaningful for you?

E. Briefly describe how your writing went today so you may refer to this later.

Take a break before going to the next chapter and the next writing experience. You may wish to read on to see how others reflected on their writing experience, or you may wish to relax and not think about writing right now. Both are perfectly fine! Come back next week to begin your legacy writing experience. In the meantime, do something you love to do, and be gentle with yourself.

Reflections on Affirmative Writing

A participant responded like this.

This exercise really helped me focus and hone in on what my values are and the direction I'd like to take my business and my personal life. The goals don't seem that lofty or far off when written down and expressed in such a bold fashion. I feel like I'm already there in some ways but just needed to tell myself so. Very powerful. I love the feeling of being self-assured.

Another participant wrote.

So lovely to write that! So much better than the anything is possible scenario — much nicer to actually write what is possible and awesome and inspiring to think about what can be in my life — Thank You!

It really made me appreciate what I value and commit to moving ever in the direction of continuing towards embodying these values.

One participant reflected this way.

This experience truly did affirm not only my intentions for future goals, it also, and more dramatically, affirmed this life choice & direction I am pursuing now. It's one thing to think that what you are doing is a compilation of all the life and work experiences you have had; its another to express this in concrete terms, in blue & white in this case and to have the point be driven home by your own choice of words.

Another participant compared this writing to visualization.

*Doing this kind of visualization writing is like making a commitment to oneself. We say all the time that we want to do something or even that we intend to do it, but we often don't follow through, due to fear or other roadblocks. Putting it in writing takes us to a new level of commitment — if we go back & read it & we haven't done, we will say, "Well, why not?" The present tense makes the intention concrete, and helps avoid procrastination. **I am** makes you realize that you have the <u>capacity</u>. **I am** _____ already, right <u>now</u>!*

One participant felt a lift in energy in affirming her path.

This clarified for me that I am on the right path. There flowed an energy & excitement from my spirit through my hand and onto my paper that is almost difficult to express. It was like when my massage therapist asked me about my vision of what I wanted to accomplish by going back to school because it was stressing my body and as I talked she said my shoulders & tension disappeared. This was another confirmation today that I am on the right path — so thank you.

16

Legacy Writing

Legacy writing is a way of documenting your life
experiences, values, and opinions to share with others.
It can be a cherished gift to family and loved ones, and
healing for the writers themselves.

— Andrew Weil, MD

What will your legacy be? Do the significant people in your life know
what you have valued most, what you thought was your purpose, or what
you learned about life as you lived it? Do they know how you navigated
life's challenges, celebrated life's gifts, or how you simply enjoyed
beauty every day? Do they know you have found benefits from
challenges as well as from life's beauty? Do they know how you used
your moments of reflection to make life-course corrections? Legacy
writing answers these questions and more for others and for ourselves.

When we make explicit our values, purpose, and beliefs about our
life — as well as our desires for our dying and death — we answer
questions that others may wish to ask but can't find the words. Our
answers are rooted in our life stories of the past or life stories of
significance in the present — and in passing on our wisdom, love, and
blessings for the future. In contemporary legacy writing, as with ancient
writing, we write for generations now and generations to come. It isn't
only presidents and public figures who wish to leave a legacy — many

other people want to know how their life has made a difference, that they have influenced someone or something. Legacy writing fulfills our desire for someone to know us at a profoundly deep and personal level.

Legacy Writing Prompts

Following are three legacy writing choices. For the purpose of your six-week program, choose at least one option and write for at least twenty minutes. Later, you may decide to dedicate a longer period of time and write about more topics. Some have made such writing a project on its own. Many people report a shift in perspective when they think about how their response reflects their values and purpose.

Choice # 1: Legacy Blessing

Write a blessing for someone that promotes their happiness, well-being, and prosperity. Write for twenty minutes. In your writing, affirm their gifts and talents. Consider the milestones they will encounter in their life and offer your wisdom and support. Give permission for them to love others and to enjoy life when you are no longer with them. Let the receiver know how they have blessed you and what they mean to you.

Choice #2: Legacy of Gratitude and Joy

Write a statement of gratitude and joy about a person, specific event, or life experience. Write for twenty minutes. Describe your most joyous, wonderful, exquisite experience. Recall how you felt, what you thought, what you said, what others said to you, who was with you, and where you were. How do you feel about it now?

Choice #3: Legacy Narrative

Write a short story about yourself on one of the topics below. Write for twenty minutes. Repeat as often as desired.

- Your rites of passage

- What an important experience taught you
- How something changed your life
- Your dreams attained
- Your frustrated dreams
- Your fondest memories
- Things you looked forward to in the past and things you look forward to now
- How you handle the difference between expectations, challenges, and frustrations
- What makes you get up in the morning
- What keeps you up at night
- How you unwind or how you don't
- What makes you resilient
- What five words you wish people would use when they describe you

Post-Writing Survey — Legacy Writing Assignment

Congratulations! You have completed your Legacy Writing experience. Please answer the following questionnaire. Put a number between 0 and 10 from the scale next to each question.

0	1	2	3	4	5	6	7	8	9	10
Not at all					Somewhat					A great deal

_____ A. To what degree did you express your deepest thoughts and feelings?

_____ B. To what degree do you currently feel sad or upset?

_____ C. To what degree do you currently feel happy?

_____ D. To what degree was today's writing valuable and meaningful for you?

E. Briefly describe how your writing went today so you may refer to this later.

Reflections on Legacy Writing

Blessed by blessings: Several participants share the benefits of writing a blessing.

Writing a blessing to my oldest son with whom I have had a challenging relationship was valuable and healing. It was a wonderful experience to express to him how precious he is to me. And it was empowering to me — turns out it was a blessing to me to write this and remember I am a great mom!

I very much love this ... to bless someone we love. How often are we given permission to reveal our deepest heart on paper? I can see many possibilities for legacy writing in my life. It makes me happier to write these feelings and to anticipate the responses of the recipients.

This felt wonderful. I immediately struggled with deciding who to write to. It's something I found I really wanted to do a lot of but the actual writing of it felt great. I wish I had more time but seeing how important it felt to take the time to say these things, I will continue this letter in the future and hopefully embark on the others that originally called to me as well.

I didn't know who I'd write the letter to but just dove in with my sister who has attempted suicide after surgeries and is better at the moment. I wanted to convey to her, while it may appear the opposite, that she has been my teacher. I'm surprised by what emerges once I start writing and this time I found myself bathed in feelings of gratitude and love. And I am grateful for that.

The five words I chose to be remembered by really are the core values of my life. A simple but profound exercise that prompts you to distill the essence of your being into five little words. The letter of blessing was also meaningful in that it brought forth gratitude in my heart for a person that I haven't seen in over 34 years but who was one of my best friends.

Participants felt both a sense of closure and a way to go forward.

Overwhelming stimulation but a lot to carry away from this experience. Today's writing felt like the culmination of five weeks... a framework to think about our lives and its meaning. These final questions, approaches, assignments are a great resource to continue our journey.

Legacy writing opened a window that showcased the most important things in my life. I was able to see with clarity what matters to me and why and I would like to share that with my loved ones. It was a great experience perfect for the completion of the course.

17

Conclusions

In our ending is our beginning. Now our journey together has reached a turning point. You have completed the six-week program Transform Your Health: Writing to Heal. By participating, you accepted a personal invitation to express what may have been abstract and hidden. You've been given a safe space to express your deepest feelings in a way that was insightful. We've aimed to provide a safe context for you to make sense of an emotional upheaval and find movement from trauma to affirmation by connecting your past, present, and future in a meaningful way.

Through writing, you paid attention to — rather than simply described — thoughts and feelings that are connected to events, people, places, and objects. You wrote to take care of emotional business, new or old or unfinished. Through metaphor and story structure, you mindfully examined ordinary daily events and mind/body connections unique to you. You found that writing affirmative statements may provide awareness and clarity about your gifts and strengths, and that writing about your legacy may enhance other positive emotional responses and may improve your feelings toward yourself and others. All in all, what you wrote may help you integrate traumatic events into a broader context of your life.

To continue this personal growth and healing, try to see your writing as a practice, much like a yoga or meditation practice, or like regularly going to the gym. Use your writing to reframe experiences, write about events from a perspective of compassion and empathy, write about everyday events with great attention to details and a spirit of mindfulness, and write your appreciation and gratitude for what many may call the little things — things we know are the only things needful.

Resources

Where to find help

If you feel that you need help beyond what this book offers, consider contacting the following people or agencies. Every moderately large city has groups or centers that can help you. If you are:

In need of help for an immediate or life-threatening situation. If you are suicidal, feel as though you are a danger to yourself or others, or feel as though you are truly falling apart, call 911.

In crisis or you need to talk to someone by phone. Most areas offer telephone crisis counselors, often called a Crisis Hotline, Community Mental Health Services, or Victim Services. If your distress is the result of a specific type of trauma, an organization with a toll-free number likely can assist you. Some current groups:

American Red Cross
Natural disasters, fires, chemical spills, community-wide disasters
800-733-2767

Depression Hotline
Depression and depressive feelings
888-379-3372

National Domestic Violence Hotline
Spouse abuse, child abuse, other forms of family violence
800-787-3224

National Organization for Victim Assistance
Victims and witnesses of crimes
800-879-6682

Rape, Abuse, and Incest National Network
Sexual abuse
800-656-4673

Suicide Awareness Voices of Education
Suicide crisis and education
800-273-8256

If you have access to a computer, dozens of crisis groups await you, offering information and people to talk with. Through any search engine, simply enter the type of crisis you are dealing with, such as "cancer diagnosis."

Additional Issues in Dealing with Traumas

Expressive writing can be a valuable tool in helping people to deal with traumas and emotional upheavals. Whereas many people can benefit greatly from writing, others don't. If after writing, you feel as though you haven't reaped any benefits or if you still need help in coping with your experience, please seek the advice of a physician, psychologist, or counselor.

Depression and post-traumatic stress disorder (PTSD)

Traumas have the potential to set off a cascade of biological changes that result in a host of mental and physical problems. If you are deeply depressed or disoriented because of a traumatic experience, writing should not be your first course of action. It is likely that your judgment of the experience has been impaired. In such a state, many people find it difficult — if not impossible — to put the many pieces of a horrible experience together.

Major depression. Most of us feel sad, upset, and down in the days after a shattering experience. However, if you have been extremely depressed for several weeks, including crying, feeling overwhelmingly sad or empty, and a having striking loss of energy, you may be experiencing a major depressive disorder. Other symptoms can include a loss of interest in pleasure, loss of appetite, insomnia, inability to concentrate, and even recurrent thoughts about death. Many people with this disorder have trouble even getting out of bed in the morning.

If you feel as though you may be suffering from major depression, see a physician, psychologist, or counselor. Many promising treatments can help you, including medication. Indeed, impressive advances in drug treatment have happened over the last fifty years. Medication can be a relatively fast way to get past some of the most devastating moods after a trauma. Once some of these symptoms have lifted, writing and other treatments can be far more effective.

Post-traumatic stress disorder. Only since the 1980s have the medical and psychological communities begun to appreciate how life-threatening traumas can produce their own sets of problems. Post-traumatic stress disorder (PTSD) may surface in the days and weeks after an extreme trauma where the person directly witnessed or experienced a life-threatening event. Car accidents, rape, robbery, and kidnapping frequently result in PTSD-related symptoms. In the weeks after the event, people with PTSD will often have vivid memories or dreams of the event. They report feeling extremely anxious much of the time, often with a sense of dread, which causes them to avoid reminders of the trauma. Other symptoms often seen with depression appear as well.

Both emotionally and socially, PTSD can debilitate people. As with major depression, PTSD is generally treatable in several ways. Both medication and psychotherapy are recommended. Once the most severe symptoms are in check, however, expressive writing may be particularly beneficial.

Need to see a physician or therapist. If you are experiencing a severe depression or symptoms of PTSD, see your physician or a psychiatrist — especially if you are open to taking medication. If you do not have a regular physician, consult the yellow pages or call your local physician referral network. If you would prefer to discuss your issues with someone, a psychologist or other licensed mental health specialist is recommended.

Reading List

Many excellent books supplement the ideas in this book. Some that we particularly recommend include:

Abercrombie, B. (2002). *Writing out the storm: Reading and writing your way through serious illness or injury*. New York: St. Martin's Press.

Adams, K. (1994). *Mightier than the sword*. New York: Warner Books.

Cameron, J. (2002). *The artist's way: A spiritual path to higher creativity*. New York: J.P. Tarcher.

Capacchione, L. (1988). *The power of your other hand*. North Hollywood, CA: Newcastle Publishing.

Davey, J. A. (2007). *Writing for wellness: A prescription of healing*. Enumclaw, WA: Idyll Arbor.

Dayton, T. (2003). *Daily affirmations for forgiving and moving on*. Deerfield Beach, FL: Health Communications, Inc.

DeSalvo, L. (2000). *Writing as a way of healing: How telling our stories transforms our lives*. Boston: Beacon Press

Dreher, H. (1995). *The immune power personality*. New York: Penguin Books.

Fox, J. (1997). *Poetic medicine: The healing art of poem-making*. New York: Jeremy P. Tarcher.

Goldberg, N. (1986). *Writing down the bones: Freeing the writer within*. Boston: Shambhala Publications.

Goleman, D. (1995). *Emotional intelligence*. New York: Bantam.

Herring, L. (2007). *Writing begins with the breath: Embodying your authentic voice*. Boston: Shambhala.

Myers, L. J. (2003). *Becoming whole: Writing your healing story*. San Diego: Healing Threads.

Pennebaker, J. W. (1997). *Opening up: The healing power of expressing emotions*. New York: Guilford.

Post-Ferrante, P. (2012). *Writing & healing: A mindful guide for cancer survivors*. New York: Hatherleigh.

Rosenthal, N. R. (2002). *The emotional revolution: How the new science of feeling can transform your life*. New York: Citadel Press.

Sapolsky, R. M. (1998). *Why zebras don't get ulcers* (revised edition). New York: Freeman.

Schneider, P. (2013). *How the light gets in: Writing as a spiritual practice.* Oxford: Oxford University Press.

Seligman, M. E. P. (2002). *Authentic happiness: Using the new positive psychology to realize your potential for lasting fulfillment.* New York: Free Press.

Zimmerman, S. (2002). *Writing to heal the soul: Transforming grief and loss through writing.* New York: Three Rivers Press.

References and Additional Scientific Readings

If you are interested in the research that supports the basic ideas of this book, some of the following papers are particularly helpful:

Affleck, G., & Tennen, H. (1996). Construing benefits from adversity: Adaptation significance and dispositional underpinnings. *Journal of Personality, 64*, 899-922.

Alpers, G. W., Winzelberg, A. J., Classen, C., Dev, P., Koopman, C., Roberts, H., et al. (2005). Evaluation of computerized text analysis in an Internet breast cancer support group. *Computers in Human Behavior, 21*, 343-358.

Ames, S. C., Patten, C. A., Offord, K. P., Pennebaker, J. W., Croghan, I. T., Tri, D. M., Stevens, S. R., & Hurt, R. D. (2005). Expressive writing intervention for young adult cigarette smokers. *Journal of Clinical Psychology, 61*, 1555-1570.

Ames, S. C., Patten, C. A., Werch, C. E., Echols, J. D., Schroeder, D. R., Stevens, S. R., Pennebaker, J. W., & Hurt, R. D. (in press). Expressive writing as a nicotine dependence treatment adjunct for young adult smokers. *Nicotine & Tobacco Research.*

Andersson, M. A., & Conley, C. S. (2013). Optimizing the perceived benefits and health outcomes of writing about traumatic events. *Stress Health, 29*(1), 40-49.

Arigo, D., & Smyth, J. M. (2012). The benefits of expressive writing on sleep difficulty and appearance concerns for college women. *Psychology & Health, 27*(2), 210-226.

Ashley, L., O'Connor, D. B., & Jones, F. (2011). Effects of emotional disclosure in caregivers: Moderating role of alexithymia. *Stress and Health, 27*(5), 376-387.

Ashley, L., O'Connor, D. B., & Jones, F. (2013). A randomized trial of written emotional disclosure interventions in school teachers: Controlling for positive expectancies and effects on health and job satisfaction. *Psychology, health & medicine, 18*(5):588-600. doi: 10.1080/13548506.2012.756536. Epub 2013 Jan 16.

Averill, A. J., Kasarskis, E. J., & Segerstrom, S. C. (2013). Expressive disclosure to improve well-being in patients with amyotrophic lateral sclerosis: A randomised, controlled trial. *Psychology & Health, 28*(6):701-13. doi: 10.1080/08870446.2012.754891. Epub 2013 Jan 7

Baddeley, J. L., & Pennebaker, J. W. (2011). A postdeployment expressive writing intervention for military couples: a randomized controlled trial. *The Journal of Trauma Stress, 24*(5), 581-585.

Baddeley, J. L., & Pennebaker, J. W. (2011). The expressive writing method. In *Research on Writing Approaches in Mental Health,* edited by L. L'Abate & L. Sweeny, 23-35. United Kingdom: Emerald.

Badger, K., Royse, D., & Moore, K. (2011). What's in a story? A text analysis of burn survivors' web-posted narratives. *Social Work in Health Care, 50*(8), 577-594.

Baikie, K. A. (2008). Who does expressive writing work for? Examination of alexithymia, splitting, and repressive coping style as moderators of the expressive writing paradigm. *British Journal of Health Psychology, 13,* 61-66.

Baikie, K. A., Geerligs, L., & Wilhelm, K. (2012). Expressive writing and positive writing for participants with mood disorders: an online randomized controlled trial. *Journal of Affective Disorders, 136*(3), 310-319.

Baikie, K. A., & Wilhelm, K. (2005). Emotional and physical health benefits of expressive writing. *Advances in Psychiatric Treatment, 11,* 338-346.

Baker, J. R., & Moore, S. M. (2008). Blogging as a social tool: a psychological examination of the effects of blogging. *CyberPsychology & Behavior, 11,* 747-74.

Barclay, L. J., & Skarlicki, D. P. (2009). Healing the wounds of organizational injustice: Examining the benefits of expressive writing. *Journal of Applied Psychology, 94*(2), 511.

Barry, L. M., & Singer, G. H. S. (2001). Reducing maternal psychological distress after the NICU experience through journal writing. *Journal of Early Intervention, 24*, 287-297.

Batten, S. V., Follette, V. M., & Palm, K. M. (2002). Physical and psychological effects of written disclosure among sexual abuse survivors. *Behavior Therapy, 33*, 107-122.

Baum, E. S., & Rude, S. S. (2013). Acceptance-enhanced expressive writing prevents symptoms in participants with low initial depression. *Cognitive Therapy and Research, 37*(1), 35-42.

Beckwith, K. M., Greenberg, M. A., & Gevirtz, R. (2005). Autonomic effects of expressive writing in individuals with elevated blood pressure. *Journal of Health Psychology, 10*, 197-209.

Bernard, M., Jackson, C., & Jones, C. (2006). Written emotional disclosure following first-episode psychosis: Effects on symptoms of post-traumatic stress disorder. *British Journal of Clinical Psychology, 45*, 403-415.

Blechinger, T., & Klosinski, G. (2011). The meaning of bibliotherapy and expressive writing in child and adolescent psychiatry. *Praxis der Kinderpsychologie und Kinderpsychiatrie, 60*(2), 109-124.

Boals, A. (2012). The use of meaning making in expressive writing: When meaning is beneficial. *Journal of Social and Clinical Psychology, 31*(4), 393-409.

Boals, A., Banks, J. B., & Hayslip Jr., B. (2012). A self-administered, mild form of exposure therapy for older adults. *Aging & Mental Health, 16*(2), 154-161.

Bolton, G., Howlett, S., Lago, C., & Wright, J. K. (Eds.) (2004). Writing cures: An introductory handbook of writing in counselling and therapy. New York: Brunner-Routledge.

Bond, M., & Pennebaker, J. W. (2012). Automated computer-based feedback in expressive writing. *Computers in Human Behavior, 28*(3), 1014-1018.

Booth, R. J., & Davison, K. P. (2003). Relating to our worlds in a psychobiological context: The impact of disclosure on self-generation and immunity. In J. Wilce (Ed.), *Social and Cultural Lives of Immune Systems* (pp. 36-48). London and New York: Routledge.

Booth, R. J., Petrie, K. J., & Pennebaker, J. W. (1997). Changes in circulating lymphocyte numbers following emotional disclosure: Evidence of buffering? *Stress Medicine, 13*, 23-29.

Bornstein, R. F. (2010). Gender schemas, gender roles, and expressive writing: Toward a process-focused model. *Sex roles, 63*(3-4), 173-177.

Bower, J. E., Kemeny, M. E., Taylor, S. E., & Fahey, J. L. (2003). Finding meaning and its association with natural killer cell cytotoxicity among participants in a bereavement-related disclosure intervention. *Annals of Behavioral Medicine, 25*, 146-155.

Brewin, C.R. & Lennard, H. (1999). Effects of mode of writing on emotional narratives. *Journal of Traumatic Stress, 12*, 355-361.

Broderick, J. E., Junghaenel, D. U., & Schwartz, J. E. (2005). Written emotional expression produces health benefits in fibromyalgia patients. *Psychosomatic Medicine, 67*, 326-334.

Broderick, J. E., Stone, A. A., Smyth, J. M., Kaell, A. T. (2004). The feasibility and effectiveness of an expressive writing intervention for rheumatoid arthritis via home-based videotaped instructions. *Annals of Behavioral Medicine, 27*, 50-59.

Brown, E. J. & Heimberg, R. G. (2001). Effects of writing about rape: Evaluating Pennebaker's paradigm with a severe trauma. *Journal of Traumatic Stress, 14*, 781.

Burke, P. A., & Bradley, R. G. (2006). Language use in imagined dialogue and narrative disclosures of trauma. *Journal of Traumatic Stress, 1*, 141-146.

Bursch, H. C., & Butcher, H. K. (2012). Caregivers' deepest feelings in living with Alzheimer's disease: a Ricoeurian interpretation of family caregivers' journals. *Research in Gerontological Nursing, 5*(3), 207-215.

Burton, C. M., & King. L. A. (2004). The health benefits of writing about intensely positive experiences. *Journal of Research in Personality, 38*, 150-163.

Burton, C. M., & King, L. A. (2008). Effects of (very) brief writing on health: The two-minute miracle. *British Journal of Health Psychology, 13*, 9-14.

Cameron, L. D., & Nicholls, G. (1998). Expression of stressful experiences through writing: Effects of a self-regulation manipulation for pessimists and optimists. *Health Psychology, 17*, 84-92.

Campbell, R. S. & Pennebaker, J. W. (2003). The secret life of pronouns: Flexibility in writing style and physical health. *Psychological Science, 14*, 60-65.

Carmack, C. L., Basen-Engquist, K., Yuan, Y., Greisinger, A., Rodriguez-Bigas, M., Wolff, R. A., ... & Pennebaker, J. W. (2011). Feasibility of an expressive-disclosure group intervention for post-treatment colorectal cancer patients. *Cancer, 117*(21), 4993-5002.

Carretti, B., Re, A. M., & Arfe, B. (2013). Reading comprehension and expressive writing: a comparison between good and poor comprehenders. *Journal of Learning Disabilities, 46*(1), 87-96.

Casey, C. Y., Greenberg, M. A., Nicassio, P. M., Harpin, R. E., & Hubbard, D. (2007, in press). Transition from acute to chronic pain and disability: A model including cognitive, affective, and trauma factors. *Pain, 134*(1-2):69-79. Epub 2007 May 15

Chaudoir, S. R., & Fisher, J. D. (2010). The disclosure processes model: Understanding disclosure decision making and postdisclosure outcomes among people living with a concealable stigmatized identity. *Psychological Bulletin, 136*(2), 236.

Cho, S., Bernstein, K. S., Cho, S., & Roh, S. (2012). Logo-autobiography and its effectiveness on depressed Korean immigrant women: A replication study. *Journal of Nursing Education and Practice, 3*(6), p51.

Christensen ,A. J., Edwards, D. L., Wiebe, J. S., Benotsch, E. G., McKelvey, L., Andrews, M., & Lubaroff, D. M. (1996). Effect of verbal self-disclosure on natural killer cell activity: Moderating influence of cynical hostility. *Psychosomatic Medicine, 58*, 150-155.

Christensen, A. J. & Smith, T. W. (1993). Cynical hostility and cardiovascular reactivity during self-disclosure. *Psychosomatic Medicine, 55,* 193-202.

Chung, C. K., & Pennebaker, J. W. (2008). Variations in spacing of expressive writing sessions. *British Journal of Health Psychology, 13*, 15-21.

Cohen, G. L., Garcia, J., Apfel, N., & Master, A. (2006). Reducing the racial achievement gap: A social-psychological intervention. *Science, 313*, 1307-1310.

Cole, S. W., Kemeny, M. E., Taylor, S. E., Visscher, B. R., & Fahey, J. L. (1996). Accelerated course of human immunodeficiency virus infection in gay men who conceal their homosexual identity. *Psychosomatic Medicine, 58,* 219-231.

Comprone, J. C., & Ronald, K. J. (2010). Expressive writing: Exercises in a new progymnasmata. *Journal of Teaching Writing, 4*(1), 31-54.

Consedine, N. S., Krivoshekova, Y. S., & Magai, C. (2012). Play it (again) Sam: Linguistic changes predict improved mental and physical health among older adults. *Journal of Language and Social Psychology, 31*(3), 240-262.

Cornoldi, C., Del Prete, F., Gallani, A., Sella, F., & Re, A. M. (2010). Components affecting expressive writing in typical and disabled writers. *Advances in Learning and Behavioral Disabilities, 23*, 269-286.

Corter, A., & Petrie, K. J. (2011). Expressive writing in patients diagnosed with cancer. In *Emotion Regulation and Well-Being,* edited by I. Nyklíček, A. J. J. M. Vingerhoets, & M. Zeelenberg, 297-306. New York: Springer.

Craft, M. A., Davis, G. C., & Paulson, R. M. (2013). Expressive writing in early breast cancer survivors. *Journal of Advanced Nursing, 69*(2), 305-315.

Creswell, J. D., Lam, S., Stanton, A. L., Taylor, S. E., Bower, J. E., & Sherman, D. K. (2007). Does self-affirmation, cognitive processing, or discovery of meaning explain cancer-related health benefits of expressive writing? *Personality & Social Psychology Bulletin, 33*, 238-250.

Cusinato, M., & L'Abate, L. (2012). *Advances in relational competence theory: With special attention to alexithymia.* Nova Science Publishers.

Culp, M. B., & Spann, S. (2010). The influence of writing on reading. *Journal of Teaching Writing, 4*(2), 284-289.

Dalton, J. J., & Glenwick, D. S. (2009). Effects of expressive writing on standardized graduate entrance exam performance and physical health functioning. *The Journal of Psychology, 143*(3), 279-292.

Danoff-Burg, S., Mosher, C. E., Seawell, A. H., & Agee, J. D. (2010). Does narrative writing instruction enhance the benefits of expressive writing? *Anxiety, Stress, & Coping, 23*(3), 341-352.

Davis, C. G., & McKearney, J. M. (2003). How do people grow from their experience with trauma or loss? *Journal of Social and Clinical Psychology, 22*, 477-492.

De Giacomo, P., L'Abate, L., Pennebaker, J. W., & Rumbaugh, D. (2010). Amplifications and applications of Pennebaker's analogic to digital model in health promotion, prevention, and psychotherapy. *Clinical Psychology & Psychotherapy, 17*(5), 355-362.

De Moor, C., Sterner, J., Hall, M., Warneke, C., Gilani, Z., Amato, R., et al. (2002). A pilot study of the effects of expressive writing on psychological and behavioral adjustment in patients enrolled in a phase II trial of vaccine therapy for metastatic renal cell carcinoma. *Health Psychology, 21*, 615-619.

Deacon, B. J., Lickel, J. J., Possis, E. A., Abramowitz, J. S., Mahaffey, B., & Wolitzky-Taylor, K. (2012). Do cognitive reappraisal and diaphragmatic breathing augment interoceptive exposure for anxiety sensitivity? *Journal of Cognitive Psychotherapy, 26*(3), 257-269.

DeMarco, R. F., & Chan, K. (2013). The Sistah Powah structured writing intervention: A feasibility study for aging, low-income, HIV-positive black women. *American Journal of Health Promotion. 28*(2):108-18. doi: 10.4278/ajhp.120227-QUAN-115. Epub 2013 Apr 26.

Deters, P. B., & Range, L. M. (2003). Does writing reduce posttraumatic stress disorder symptoms? *Violence and Victims, 18*, 569-580.

Dolev-Cohen, M., & Barak, A. (2012). Adolescents' use of Instant Messaging as a means of emotional relief. *Computers in Human Behavior.* 29(1), 58 –63. http://dx.doi.org/10.1016/j.chb.2012.07.016

Donnelly, D. A., & Murray, E. J. (1991). Cognitive and emotional changes in written essays and therapy interviews. *Journal of Social and Clinical Psychology, 10,* 334-350.

Drake, J. E., & Winner, E. (2012). How children use drawing to regulate their emotions. *Cognition & Emotion, 27*(3):512-20. doi: 10.1080/02699931.2012.720567. Epub 2012 Sep 11.

Dube, S. R., Fairweather, D., Pearson, W. S., Felitti, V. J., Anda, R. F., & Croft, J. B. (2009). Cumulative childhood stress and autoimmune diseases in adults. *Psychosomatic Medicine, 71*(2), 243-250.

Earnhardt, J. L., Martz, D. M., Ballard, M. E., & Curtin, L. (2002). A writing intervention for negative body image: Pennebaker fails to surpass the placebo. *Journal of College Student Psychotherapy, 17*, 19-35.

East, P., Startup, H., Roberts, C., & Schmidt, U. (2010). Expressive writing and eating disorder features: A preliminary trial in a student sample of the impact of three writing tasks on eating disorder symptoms and associated cognitive, affective and interpersonal factors. *European Eating Disorders Review, 18*(3), 180-196.

Ellis, D. & Cromby, J. (2009) Inhibition and reappraisal within emotional disclosure: the embodying of narration. *Counselling Psychology Quarterly, 22*, 319-331.

Engelhard, G., Jr., & Behizadeh, N. (2012). Exploring the alignment of writing self-efficacy with writing achievement using Rasch measurement theory and qualitative methods. *Journal of Applied Measurement, 13*(2), 132-145.

Epstein, E. M., Sloan, D. M., & Marx, B. P. (2005). Getting to the heart of the matter: Written disclosure, gender, and heart rate. *Psychosomatic Medicine, 67*, 413-419

Esterling, B. A., Antoni, M. H., Fletcher, M. A., Margulies, S., & Schneiderman, N. (1994). Emotional disclosure through writing or speaking modulates latent Epstein-Barr virus antibody titers. *Journal of Consulting and Clinical Psychology, 62,* 130-140.

Facchin, F., Margola, D., Molgora, S., & Revenson, T. A. (2013). Effects of benefit-focused versus standard expressive writing on adolescents' self-concept during the high school transition. *Journal of Research on Adolescence.* online: 25 MAR 2013 http://onlinelibrary.wiley.com/doi/10.1111/jora.12040/abstract

Felitti, V. J., Anda, R. F., Nordenberg, D., Williamson, D. F., Spitz, A. M., Edwards, V., ... & Marks, J. S. (1998). The relationship of adult health status to childhood abuse and household dysfunction. *American Journal of Preventive Medicine, 14*(4), 245-258.

Fernandez, I., Paez, D., & Pennebaker, J. W. (2009). Comparison of expressive writing after the terrorist attacks of September 11th and March 11th. *International Journal of Clinical and Health Psychology, 9*, 89-103.

Fivush, R., Marin, K., Crawford, M., Reynolds, M., & Brewin, C. R. (2007). Children's narratives and well-being. *Cognition and Emotion, 21*, 1414-1434.

Floyd, K., Mikkelson, A. C., Hesse, C., & Pauley, P. M. (2007). Affectionate writing reduces total cholesterol: Two randomized controlled trials. *Human Communication Research, 33*, 119-142.

Foa, E. B., & Meadows, E. A. (1997). Psychosocial treatments for posttraumatic stress disorder: a critical review. *Annual Review of Psychology, 48*, 449-480.

Francis, M. E. & Pennebaker, J. W. (1992). Putting stress into words: Writing about personal upheavals and health. *American Journal of Health Promotion, 6*, 280-287.

Frattaroli, J. (2006). Experimental disclosure and its moderators: A meta-analysis. *Psychological Bulletin, 132*, 823-865.

Frattaroli, J., Thomas, M., & Lyubomirsky, S. (2011). Opening up in the classroom: effects of expressive writing on graduate school entrance exam performance. *Emotion, 11*(3), 691-696.

Frayne, A., & Wade, T. D. (2006). A comparison of written emotional expression and planning with respect to bulimic symptoms and associated psychopathology. *European Eating Disorders Review, 14*, 329-340.

Fredrickson, B. (2009). *Positivity: Top-notch research reveals the 3 to 1 ratio that will change your life.* Random House Digital, Inc..

Freyd, J. J., Klest, B., & Allard, C. B. (2005). Betrayal trauma: Relationship to physical health, psychological distress, and a written disclosure intervention. *Journal of Trauma & Dissociation, 6*, 83-104.

Frisina, P. G., Borod, J. C., & Lepore, S. J. (2004). A meta-analysis of the effects of written emotional disclosure on the health outcomes of clinical populations. *Journal of Nervous and Mental Disease, 192*, 629-634.

Furnes, B., & Dysvik, E. (2010). A systematic writing program as a tool in the grief process: part 1. *Patient Preference and Adherence, 4*, 425-431.

Gallagher, P., & MacLachlan, M. (2002). Evaluating a written emotional disclosure homework intervention for lower-limb amputees. *Archives of Physical and Medical Rehabilitation, 83*, 1464-1466.

Gallant, M. D., & Lafreniere, K. D. (2003). Effects of an emotional disclosure writing task on the physical and psychological functioning of children of alcoholics. *Alcoholism Treatment Quarterly, 21*, 55-66.

Gamber, A. M., Lane-Loney, S., & Levine, M. P. (2013). Effects and linguistic analysis of written traumatic emotional disclosure in an eating-disordered population. *The Permanente Journal, 17*(1), 16.

Gellaitry, G., Peters, K., Bloomfield, D., & Horne, R. (2010). Narrowing the gap: The effects of an expressive writing intervention on perceptions of actual and ideal emotional support in women who have completed treatment for early stage breast cancer. *Psycho-Oncology, 19*(1), 77-84.

Gidron, Y., Duncan, E., Lazar, A., Biderman, A., Tandeter, H., & Shvartzman, P. (2002). Effects of guided disclosure of stressful experiences on clinic visits and symptoms in frequent clinic attenders. *Family Practice, 19*, 161-166.

Gidron, Y., Gal, R., Freedman, S., Twiser, I., Lauden, A., Snir, Y., & Benjamin, J. (2001). Translating research findings to PTSD prevention: Results of a randomized-controlled pilot study, *Journal of Traumatic Stress, 14*, 773-780.

Gidron, Y., Peri, T., Connolly, J. F., & Shalev, A. Y. (1996). Written disclosure in posttraumatic stress disorder: Is it beneficial for the patient? *Journal of Nervous & Mental Disease, 184*, 505- 507.

Gillam, T. (2010). The therapeutic value of writing. *British Journal of Wellbeing, 1*(6), 27.

Gillis, M. E., Lumley, M. A., Mosley-Williams, A., Leisen, J. C. C., & Roehrs, T. (in press). The health effects of at-home written emotional disclosure in fibromyalgia: A randomized trial. *Annals of Behavioral Medicine*.

Gortner, E., Rude, S., & Pennebaker, J. W. (2006). Benefits of expressive writing in lowering rumination and depressive symptoms. *Behavior Therapy, 37*, 292-303

Graybeal, A., Seagal, J. D., & Pennebaker, J. W. (2002). The role of story-making in disclosure writing: The psychometrics of narrative. *Psychology and Health, 17*, 571-581.

Greenberg, M. A., & Stone, A. A. (1992). Emotional disclosure about traumas and its relation to health: Effects of previous disclosure and trauma severity. *Journal of Personality and Social Psychology, 63*, 75-84.

Greenberg, M. A., Stone, A. A., & Wortman, C. B. (1996). Health and psychological effects of emotional disclosure: A test of the inhibition-confrontation approach. *Journal of Personality and Social Psychology, 71*, 588-602.

große Deters, F., & Mehl, M. R. (2012). Does posting Facebook status updates increase or decrease loneliness? An online social networking experiment. *Social Psychological and Personality Science*.

Guinther, P. M., Segal, D. L., & Bogaards, J. A. (2003). Gender differences in emotional processing among bereaved older adults. *Journal of Loss and Trauma, 8*, 15-33.

Halpert, A., Rybin, D., & Doros, G. (2010). Expressive writing is a promising therapeutic modality for the management of IBS: a pilot study. *American Journal of Gastroenterology, 105*(11), 2440-2448.

Hamilton-West, K. E., & Quine, L. (2007). Effects of written emotional disclosure on health outcomes in patients with ankylosing spondylitis. *Psychology and Health, 22*, 637-657.

Harber, K. D., & Cohen, D. (2005). The emotional broadcaster theory of social sharing. *Journal of Language and Social Psychology, 24*, 382-400.

Harber, K. D., Einav-Cohen, M., & Lang, F. (in press). They heard a cry: Psycho-social resources moderate perception of others' distress. *European Journal of Social Psychology*.

Harber, K. D., & Wenberg, K. E. (2005). Emotional disclosure and closeness to offenders. *Personality and Social Psychology Bulletin, 31*, 734-746.

Harris, A. H. (2006). Does expressive writing reduce health care utilization? A meta-analysis of randomized trials. *Journal of Consultative Clinical Psychology, 74*(2), 243-252.

Harris, A. H. S., Thoresen, C. E., Humpheys, K., & Faul, J. (2005). Does expressive writing affect asthma? A randomized trial. *Psychosomatic Medicine, 67*, 130-136.

Harvey, A. G. & Farrel, C. (2003). The efficacy of the Pennebaker-like writing intervention for poor sleepers. *Behavioral Sleep Medicine, 1*, 115-124.

Hemenover, S. H. (2003). The good, the bad, and the healthy: Impacts of emotional disclosure of trauma on resilient self-concept and psychological distress, *Personality and Social Psychology Bulletin, 29*, 1236-1244.

Henry, E. A., Schlegel, R. J., Talley, A. E., Molix, L. A., & Bettencourt, B. A. (2010). The feasibility and effectiveness of expressive writing for rural and urban breast cancer survivors. *Oncology Nursing Forum, 37*(6), 749-757.

Hevey, D., Wilczkiewicz, E., & Horgan, J. H. (2012). Type D moderates the effects of expressive writing on health-related quality of life (HRQOL) following myocardial infarction (MI). *The Irish Journal of Psychology, 33*(2-3), 107-114.

Hijazi, A. M., Tavakoli, S., Slavin-Spenny, O. M., & Lumley, M. A. (2011). Targeting interventions: moderators of the effects of expressive writing and assertiveness training on the adjustment of international university students. *International Journal of Advanced Counseling, 33*(2), 101-112.

Hirai, M., Skidmore, S. T., Clum, G. A., & Dolma, S. (2012). An investigation of the efficacy of online expressive writing for trauma-related psychological distress in Hispanic individuals. *Behavioral Therapy, 43*(4), 812-824.

Hockemeyer, J., Smyth, J., Anderson, C., & Stone, A. (1999). Is it safe to write? Evaluating the short-term distress produced by writing about emotionally traumatic experiences. *Psychosomatic Medicine, 61* [Abstract]

Hölzel, B. K., Carmody, J., Evans, K. C., Hoge, E. A., Dusek, J. A., Morgan, L., Pitman, R. K., & Lazar, S. W. (2010). Stress reduction correlates with structural changes in the amygdala. *Social Cognitive Affective Neuroscience, 5*(1), 11-17.

Honos-Webb, L., Harrick, E. A., Stiles, W. B., & Park, C. (2000). Assimilation of traumatic experiences and physical-health outcomes: Cautions for the Pennebaker paradigm. *Psychotherapy, 37*, 307-314.

Horn, A. B., & Mehl, M. R. (2004). Expressives Schreiben als Copingtechnik: Ein Überblick über den Stand der Forschung. *Verhaltenstherapie, 14*, 274-283.

Horn, A. B., Possel, P., & Hautzinger, M. (2011). Promoting adaptive emotion regulation and coping in adolescence: a school-based programme. *Journal of Health Psychology, 16*(2), 258-273.

Hoyt, M. A., Stanton, A. L., Bower, J. E., Thomas, K. S., Litwin, M. S., Breen, E. C., & Irwin, M. R. (2013). Inflammatory biomarkers and emotional approach coping in men with prostate cancer. *Brain, Behavior, and Immunity. 31.* 173-179. http://dx.doi.org/10.1016/j.bbi.2013.04.008.

Hoyt, T., & Yeater, E. A. (2011). The effects of negative emotion and expressive writing on posttraumatic stress symptoms. *Journal of Social and Clinical Psychology, 30*(6), 549-569.

Hsu, M. C., Schubiner, H., Stracks, J. S., & Clauw, D. J. (2010). Sustained pain reduction through affective self-awareness in fibromyalgia: a randomized controlled trial. *Journal of General Internal Medicine, 25*(10), 1064-1070.

Imrie, S., & Troop, N. A. (2012). A pilot study on the effects and feasibility of compassion-focused expressive writing in day hospice patients. *Palliative and Supportive Care,* doi:10.1017/S1478951512000181

Ironson, G., O'Cleirigh, C., Leserman, J., Stuetzle, R., Fordiani, J., Fletcher, M., & Schneiderman, N. (2013). Gender-specific effects of an augmented written emotional disclosure intervention on posttraumatic, depressive, and HIV-disease-related outcomes: a randomized, controlled trial. *Journal of Consultative Clinical Psychology, 81*(2), 284-298.

Jacobson, L. T., & Reid, R. (2012). Improving the writing performance of high school students with Attention Deficit/Hyperactivity Disorder and writing difficulties. *Exceptionality, 20*(4), 218-234.

Jensen-Johansen, M. B., Christensen, S., Valdimarsdottir, H., Zakowski, S., Jensen, A. B., Bovbjerg, D. H., & Zachariae, R. (2012). Effects of an expressive writing intervention on cancer-related distress in Danish breast cancer survivors: results from a nationwide randomized clinical trial. *Psycho-Oncology, 22*, 1492-1500.

Johnston, O., Startup, H., Lavender, A., Godfrey, E., & Schmidt, U. (2010). Therapeutic writing as an intervention for symptoms of bulimia nervosa: Effects and mechanism of change. *International Journal of Eating Disorders, 43*(5), 405-419.

Joseph, L. M., & Greenberg, M. A. (2001). The effects of a career transition program on reemployment success in laid-off professionals. *Consulting Psychology Journal, 53*, 169-181.

Kalantari, M., Yule, W., Dyregrov, A., Neshatdoost, H., & Ahmadi, S. J. (2012). Efficacy of writing for recovery on traumatic grief symptoms of Afghani refugee bereaved adolescents: a randomized control trial. *OMEGA — Journal of Death and Dying, 65*(2), 139-150.

Kaptein, A. A., Lyons, A. C., Pearson, A. S., van der Geest, S., Haan, J., Meulenberg, F., & Smyth, J. M. (2012). Storying stories. *Medical Education Development, 2*(1), e7.

Kearns, M. C., Edwards, K. M., Calhoun, K. S., & Gidycz, C. A. (2010). Disclosure of sexual victimization: The effects of Pennebaker's emotional disclosure paradigm on physical and psychological distress. *Journal of Trauma & Dissociation, 11*(2), 193-209.

Kelley J. E., Lumley M. A., Leisen J. C. (1997). Health effects of emotional disclosure in rheumatoid arthritis patients. *Health Psychology, 16*, 331-340.

Kellogg, R. T., Mertz, H. K., & Morgan, M. (2010). Do gains in working memory capacity explain the written self-disclosure effect? *Cognition and Emotion, 24*(1), 86-93.

Kelly, A. E., Klusas, J. A., von Weiss, R. T., & Kenny, C. (2001). What is it about revealing secrets that is beneficial? *Personality and Social Psychology Bulletin, 27*, 651-665.

Kelly, R. E., Wood, A. M., Shearman, K., Phillips, S., & Mansell, W. (2012). Encouraging acceptance of ambivalence using the expressive writing paradigm. *Psychology and Psychotherapy: Theory, Research and Practice, 85*(2), 220-228.

Kim, Y. (2008). Effects of expressive writing among bilinguals: exploring psychological well-being and social behaviour. *British Journal of Health Psychology, 13*(Pt 1), 43-47.

King, L. A. (2001). The health benefits of writing about life goals. *Personality and Social Psychology Bulletin, 27*, 798-807.

King, L. A. & Miner, K. N. (2000). Writing about the perceived benefits of traumatic events: Implications for physical health. *Personality and Social Psychology Bulletin, 26*, 220-230.

Kirk, B. A., Schutte, N. S., & Hine, D. W. (2011). The effect of an expressive-writing intervention for employees on emotional self-efficacy, emotional intelligence, affect, and workplace incivility. *Journal of Applied Social Psychology, 41*(1), 179-195.

Klapow, J. C., Schmidt, S. M., Taylor, L. A., Roller, P., Li, Q., Calhoun, J. W., Wallander, J., & Pennebaker, J. W. (2001). Symptom management in older primary care patients: Feasibility of an experimental, written self-disclosure protocol. *Annals of Internal Medicine, 134*, 905-911.

Klein, K., & Boals, A. (2001). Expressive writing can increase working memory capacity. *Journal of Experimental Psychology: General, 130*, 520-533.

Kliewer, W., Lepore, S. J., Farrell, A. D., Allison, K. W., Meyer, A. L., Sullivan, T. N., & Greene, A. Y. (2011). A school-based expressive writing intervention for at-risk urban adolescents' aggressive behavior and emotional lability. *Journal of Clinical Child Adolescent Psychology, 40*(5), 693-705.

Kloss, J.D., & Lisman, S. A. (2002). An exposure-based examination of the effects of written emotional disclosure. *British Journal of Health Psychology, 7*, 31-46.

Knowles, E. D., Wearing, J. R., & Campos, B. (2011). Culture and the health benefits of expressive writing. *Social Psychological and Personality Science, 2*(4), 408-415.

Ko, H.-C., & Kuo, F.-Y. (in press). Can blogging enhance subjective well-being through self-disclosure? *CyberPsychology & Behavior.*

Koopman, C., Ismailji, T., Holmes, D., Classen, C. C., Palesh, O., & Wales, T. (2005). The effects of expressive writing on pain, depression and posttraumatic stress disorder symptoms in survivors of intimate partner violence. *Journal of Health Psychology, 10*(2), 211-221.

Koschwanez, H. E., Kerse, N., Darragh, M., Jarrett, P., Booth, R. J., & Broadbent, E. (2013). Expressive writing and wound healing in older adults: A randomized controlled trial. *Psychosomatic Medicine, 75*(6), 581-590.

Kovac, S. H., & Range, L. M. (2000). Writing projects: Lessening undergraduates' unique suicidal bereavement. *Suicide & Life-Threatening Behavior, 30*, 50-60.

Kovac, S. H., & Range, L. M. (2002). Does writing about suicidal thoughts and feelings reduce them? *Suicide and Life-Threatening Behavior, 32*, 428-440.

Kowalski, R. M., & Cantrell, C. C. (2002). Intrapersonal and interpersonal consequences of complaints. *Representative Research in Social Psychology, 26*, 26-33.

Kraaij, V., van Emmerik, A., Garnefski, N., Schroevers, M. J., Lo-Fo-Wong, D., van Empelen, P., ... & Maes, S. (2010). Effects of a cognitive behavioral self-help program and a computerized structured writing intervention on depressed mood for HIV-infected people: A pilot randomized controlled trial. *Patient Education and Counseling, 80*(2), 200-204.

Krantz, A. M. & Pennebaker, J. W. (2007). Expressive dance, writing, trauma, and health: When words have a body. In *Whole Person Healthcare Vol 3: The Arts and Health,* edited by I. A. Serlin, J Sonke-Henderson, R. Brandman, & J. Graham-Pole, 201-229. Westport, CT: Praeger.

Kroner-Herwig, B., Linkemann, A., & Morris, L. (2004). Selbstöffnung beim Schreiben über belastende Lebensereignisse: Ein Weg in die Gesundheit? Zeitschrift für Klinische Psychologie und Psychotherapie, 33, 183 — 190. [Reprinted in English: Morris, L., Linkemann, A. & Kröner-Herwig, B. (2005). Writing your way to health? The effects of disclosure in German students. In M. E. Abelian (Ed.) *Focus on Psychotherapy Research,* 219-239. Nova Science, New York].

L'Abate, L., & Sweeney, L. G. (Eds.). (2011). *Research on writing approaches in mental health* (Vol. 23). Bingley, England: Emerald Group Publishing.

Laccetti, M. (2007). Expressive writing in women with advanced breast cancer. *Oncology Nursing Forum, 34*(5), 1019-1024.

Lange-Nielsen, I. I., Kolltveit, S., Thabet, A. A. M., Dyregrov, A., Pallesen, S., Johnsen, T. B., & Laberg, J. C. (2012). Short-term effects of a writing intervention among adolescents in Gaza. *Journal of Loss and Trauma, 17*(5), 403-422.

Lange, A, Ven, J-P. van de, Schrieken, B., & Emmelkamp, P. (2001). INTERAPY. Treatment of posttraumatic stress through the Internet: A controlled trial. *Behavioral Research and Experimental Psychiatry, 32*, 73-90.

Lange, A., Rietdijk, D., Hudcovicova, M., Van de Ven, J-P., Schrieken, S. & Emmelkamp, P. M. G. (2003). INTERAPY: A controlled randomized trial of the standardized treatment of posttraumatic stress through the Internet. *Journal of Consulting and Clinical Psychology, 71*, 901-909.

Lange, A., Schoutrop, M. J. A., Schrieken, B., & Ven, J-P. (2002). Interapy: a model for therapeutic writing through the internet. In *The writing cure: How expressive writing Promotes health and emotional well being* edited by S. J. Lepore & J. M. Smyth, Chapter 12, p.215-238. Washington: APA.

Lange, A., Ven, J-P. van de, & Schrieken, B. (in press). Interapy, treatment of posttraumatic stress and PTSD through the internet: theory, practice and research findings. *Cognitive Behaviour Therapy*.

Langens, T. A., & Schuler, J. (2005). Written emotional expression and emotional well-being: The moderating role of fear of rejection. *Personality and Social Psychology Bulletin, 31*, 818-830.

Langens, T. A., & Schuler, J. (2007). Effects of written emotional expression: The role of positive expectancies. *Health Psychology, 26*, 174-182.

Langer, S. L., Kelly, T. H., Storer, B. E., Hall, S. P., Lucas, H. G., & Syrjala, K. L. (2012). Expressive talking among caregivers of hematopoietic stem cell transplant survivors: Acceptability and concurrent subjective, objective, and physiologic indicators of emotion. *Journal of Psychosocial Oncology, 30*(3), 294-315.

Largo-Marsh, L., & Spates, C. R. (2002). The effects of writing therapy in comparison to EMD/R on traumatic stress: The relationship between hypnotizability and client expectancy to outcome. *Professional Psychology: Research & Practice, 33*, 581-586.

Leach, M. M., Greer, T., & Gaughf, J. (2010). Linguistic analysis of interpersonal forgiveness: Process trajectories. *Personality and Individual Differences, 48*(2), 117-122.

Leake, R., Friend, R., & Wadhwa, N. (1999). Improving adjustment to chronic illness through strategic self-presentation: An experimental study on a renal dialysis unit. *Health Psychology, 18*, 54-62.

Lee, H. S., & Cohn, L. D. (2010). Assessing coping strategies by analysing expressive writing samples. *Stress and Health, 26*(3), 250-260.

Lepore, S. J. (1997). Expressive writing moderates the relation between intrusive thoughts and depressive symptoms. *Journal of Personality and Social Psychology, 73*, 1030-1037.

Lepore, S. J., & Greenberg, M. A. (2002). Mending broken hearts: Effects of expressive writing on mood, cognitive processing, social adjustment and health following a relationship breakup. *Psychology and Health, 17*, 547-560.

Lepore, S., & Smyth, J. (2002). *The writing cure: How expressive writing promotes health and emotional well-being*. Washington, DC: American Psychological Association.

Lepore, S. J., Fernandez-Berrocal, P., Ragan, J., & Ramos, N. (2004). It's not that bad: Social challenges to emotional disclosure enhance adjustment to stress. *Anxiety, Stress, and Coping, 17*, 341-361.

Lepore, S. J., Silver, R. C., Wortman, C. B., & Wayment, H. A. (1996). Social constraints, intrusive thoughts, and depressive symptoms among bereaved mothers. *Journal of Personality and Social Psychology, 70*, 271-282.

Lewis, R. J., Derlega, V. J., Clarke, E. G., Kuang, J. C., Jacobs, A. M., & McElligott, M. D. (2005). An expressive writing intervention to cope with lesbian-related stress: The moderating effects of openness about sexual orientation. *Psychology of Women Quarterly, 29*, 149-157.

Lichtenthal, W. G., & Cruess, D. G. (2010). Effects of directed written disclosure on grief and distress symptoms among bereaved individuals. *Death Studies, 34*(6), 475-499.

Lichtenthal, W. G., & Neimeyer, R. A. (2012). Directed journaling to facilitate meaning-making. *Techniques in Grief Therapy*, 165.

Littrell, J. (1998). Is the reexperience of painful emotion therapeutic? *Clinical Psychology Review, 18*, 71-102.

Lorenz, T. A., Pulverman, C. S., & Meston, C. M. (2012). Sudden gains during patient-directed expressive writing treatment predicts depression reduction in women with history of childhood sexual abuse: Results from a randomized clinical trial. *Cognitive Therapy and Research, 37*(4), 690-696.

Low, C. A., Stanton, A. L., & Danoff-Burg, S. (2006). Expressive disclosure and benefit finding among breast cancer patients: mechanisms for positive health effects. *Health Psychology, 25*(2), 181-189.

Low, C. A., Stanton, A. L., Bower, J. E., & Gyllenhammer, L. (2010). A randomized controlled trial of emotionally expressive writing for women with metastatic breast cancer. *Health Psychology, 29*(4), 460-466.

Lu, Q., & Stanton, A. L. (2010). How benefits of expressive writing vary as a function of writing instructions, ethnicity and ambivalence over emotional expression. *Psychological Health, 25*(6), 669-684.

Lu, Q., Zheng, D., Young, L., Kagawa-Singer, M., & Loh, A. (2012). A pilot study of expressive writing intervention among Chinese-speaking breast cancer survivors. *Health Psychology, 31*(5), 548-551.

Lumley, M. A. (2004). Alexithymia, emotional disclosure, and health: a program of research. *Journal of Personality, 72*(6), 1271-1300.

Lumley, M. A., Leegstra, S., Provenzano, K., & Warren, V. (1999). The health effects of writing about emotional stress on physically symptomatic young adults.(abstract) *Psychosomatic Medicine, 61*, 84-130.

Lumley, M. A., Leisen, J. C., Partridge, R. T., Meyer, T. M., Radcliffe, A. M., Macklem, D. J., ... & Granda, J. L. (2011). Does emotional disclosure about stress improve health in rheumatoid arthritis? Randomized, controlled trials of written and spoken disclosure. *Pain, 152*(4), 866-877.

Lumley, M. A. & Provenzano, K. M. (2003). Stress management through emotional disclosure improves academic performance among college students with physical symptoms. *Journal of Educational Psychology, 95*, 641-649.

Lumley, M. A., Tojek, T. M., & Macklem, D. J. (2002). Effects of written emotional disclosure among repressive and alexithymic people. In *The Writing Cure: How Expressive Writing Promotes Health and Emotional Well-Being,* edited by S. J. Lepore & J. M. Smyth ,75-95. Washington, DC: American Psychological Association.

Lutgendorf, S. K., Antoni, M. H. (1999). Emotional and cognitive processing in a trauma disclosure paradigm. *Cognitive Therapy and Research, 23*, 423-440.

Lutgendorf, S. K., Antoni, M. H., Kumar, M., & Schneiderman, N. (1994). Changes in coping strategies predict EBV antibody titers following a stressor disclosure induction. *Journal of Psychosomatic Research, 38*, 63-78.

Lyubomisky, S., Sousa, L., & Dickerhoof, R. (2006). The costs and benefits of writing, talking, and thinking about life's triumphs and defeats. *Journal of Personality and Social Psychology, 90*, 692-708.

Mackenzie, C. S., Wiprzycka, U. J., Hasher, L., & Goldstein, D. (2007). Does expressive writing reduce stress and improve health for family caregivers of older adults? *The Gerontologist, 47*, 296-306.

Mackenzie, C. S., Wiprzycka, U. J., Hasher, L., & Goldstein, D. (2008). Seeing the glass half full: Optimistic expressive writing improves mental health among chronically stressed caregivers. *British Journal of Health Psychology*, *13*(1), 73-76.

MacReady, D. E., Cheung, R. M., Kelly, A. E., & Wang, L. (2011). Can public versus private disclosure cause greater psychological symptom reduction? *Journal of Social and Clinical Psychology*, *30*(10), 1015-1042.

Maestas, K. L., & Rude, S. S. (2012). The benefits of expressive writing on autobiographical memory specificity: A randomized controlled trial. *Cognitive Therapy and Research*, *36*(3), 234-246.

Manier, D. & Olivares, A. (2005). Who benefits from expressive writing? Moderator variables affecting outcomes of emotional disclosure interventions. *Counseling and Clinical Psychology Journal*, *2*, 15-28.

Mann, T. (2001). Effects of future writing and optimism on health behaviors in HIV-infected women. *Annals of Behavioral Medicine*, *23*, 26-33.

Manzoni, G. M., Castelnuovo, G., & Molinari, E. (2011). The WRITTEN-HEART study (expressive writing for heart healing): rationale and design of a randomized controlled clinical trial of expressive writing in coronary patients referred to residential cardiac rehabilitation. *Health and Quality of Life Outcomes*, *8*(9), 51.

Marlo H., Wagner M. K. (1999). Expression of negative and positive events through writing: implications for psychotherapy and health. *Psychology and Health*, *14*, 193-215.

Martino, M. L., Freda, M. F., & Camera, F. (2013). Effects of Guided Written Disclosure Protocol on mood states and psychological symptoms among parents of off-therapy acute lymphoblastic leukemia children. *Journal of Health Psychology*, *18*(6), 727-736.

Mastropieri, M. A., Scruggs, T. E., Cerar, N. I., Allen-Bronaugh, D., Thompson, C., Guckert, M., ... & Cuenca-Sanchez, Y. (2012). Fluent Persuasive Writing With Counterarguments for Students With Emotional Disturbance. *The Journal of Special Education*. doi: 10.1177/0022466912440456. April 2, 2012

Matthiesen, S., Klonoff-Cohen, H., Zachariae, R., Jensen-Johansen, M. B., Nielsen, B. K., Frederiksen, Y., ... Ingerslev, H. J. (2012). The effect of an expressive writing intervention (EWI) on stress in infertile couples undergoing assisted reproductive technology (ART) treatment: a randomized controlled pilot study. *British Journal of Health Psychology*, *17*(2), 362-378.

McAdams, D. P. (1993). *The stories we live by: personal myths and the making of the self*. New York: Morrow.

McGuire, K. M., Greenberg, M. A., & Gevirtz, R. (2005). Autonomic effects of expressive writing in individuals with elevated blood pressure. *Journal of Health Psychology*, *10*(2), 197-209.

Mendes, W. B., Reis, H., Seery, M. D., & Blascovich, J. (2003). Cardiovascular correlates of emotional expression and suppression: Do content and gender context matter? *Journal of Personality and Social Psychology*, *84*, 771-792.

Mendolia, M., & Kleck, R. E. (1993). Effects of talking about a stressful event on arousal: Does what we talk about make a difference? *Journal of Personality and Social Psychology*, *64*, 283-292.

Merrell, R. S., Hannah, D. J., Van Arsdale, A. C., Buman, M. P., & Rice, K. G. (2011). Emergent themes in the writing of perfectionists: a qualitative study. *Psychotherapy Research*, *21*(5), 510-524.

Miranda, A., Baixauli, I., & Colomer, C. (2013). Narrative writing competence and internal state terms of young adults clinically diagnosed with childhood attention deficit hyperactivity disorder. *Research in Developmental Disabilities*, *34*(6), 1938-1950.

Moberly, N. J., & Watkins, E. R. (2006). Processing mode influences the relationship between trait rumination and emotional vulnerability. *Behavioral Therapy*, *37*(3), 281-291.

Mogk, C., Otte, S., Reinhold-Hurley, B., & Kroner-Herwig, B. (2006). Health effects of expressive writing on stressful or traumatic experiences: a meta-analysis. *GMS Psychosocial Medicine*, *3*.

Moni, R. W., Moni, K. B., Lluka, L. J., & Poronnik, P. (2007). The personal response: A novel writing assignment to engage first year students in large human biology classes. *Biochemical and Molecular Biology Education, 35*(2), 89-96.

Monin, J. K., Schulz, R., Lemay Jr., E. P., & Cook, T. B. (2012). Linguistic markers of emotion regulation and cardiovascular reactivity among older caregiving spouses. *Psychology and aging, 27*(4), 903.

Morgan, N. P., Graves, K. D., Poggi, E. A., & Cheson, B. D. (2008). Implementing an expressive writing study in a cancer clinic. *Oncologist, 13*(2), 196-204.

Morisano, D., Hirsh, J. B., Peterson, J. B., Shore, B., & Pihl, R. O. (2010). Personal goal setting, reflection, and elaboration improves academic performance in university students. *Journal of Applied Psychology, 95*, 255-264.

Morrow, J. A., Clayman, S., & McDonagh, B. (2012). In their own voices: Trauma survivors' experiences in overcoming childhood trauma. *SAGE Open, 2*(1).

Mosher, C. E., & DuHamel, K. N. (2012). An examination of distress, sleep, and fatigue in metastatic breast cancer patients. *Psycho-Oncology, 21*(1), 100-107.

Mosher, C. E., DuHamel, K. N., Lam, J., Dickler, M., Li, Y., Massie, M. J., & Norton, L. (2012). Randomised trial of expressive writing for distressed metastatic breast cancer patients. *Psychological Health, 27*(1), 88-100.

Murray, E. J., & Segal, D. L. (1994). Emotional processing in vocal and written expression of feelings about traumatic experiences. *Journal of Traumatic Stress, 7*, 391-405.

Murray, E. J., Lamnin, A. D., & Carver, C. S. (1989). Emotional expression in written essays and psychotherapy. *Journal of Social and Clinical Psychology, 8*, 414-429.

Murray, M. (2009). Health psychology and writing: an introduction. *Journal of Health Psychology, 14*(2), 158-160.

Nazarian, D., & Smyth, J. M. (2010). Context moderates the effects of an expressive writing intervention: a randomized two-study replication and extension. *Journal of Social and Clinical Psychology, 29*(8), 903-929.

Nazarian, D., & Smyth, J. M. (2013). An experimental test of instructional manipulations in expressive writing interventions: Examining processes of change. *Journal of Social and Clinical Psychology, 32*(1), 71-96.

Nicholls, S. (2009). Beyond expressive writing: Evolving models of developmental creative writing. *Journal of Health Psychology, 14*, 171-180.

Njus, D. M., Nitschke, W., & Bryant, F. B. (1996). Positive affect, negative affect, and the moderating effect of writing on sIgA antibody levels. *Psychology and Health, 12*, 135-148.

Norman, S. A., Lumley, M.A., Dooley, J. A., & Diamond, M. P. (2004). For whom does it work? Moderators of the effects of written emotional disclosure in women with chronic pelvic pain. *Psychosomatic Medicine, 66*, 174-183.

North, R. J., Pai, A. V., Hixon, J. G., & Holahan, C. J. (2011). Finding happiness in negative emotions: An experimental test of a novel expressive writing paradigm. *The Journal of Positive Psychology, 6*(3), 192-203.

O'Connor, D. B., & Ashley, L. (2008). Are alexithymia and emotional characteristics of disclosure associated with blood pressure reactivity and psychological distress following written emotional disclosure? *British Journal of Health Psychology, 13, 495-512.*

O'Connor, D. B., Hurling, R., Hendrickx, H., Osborne, G., Hall, J., Walklet, E., ... Wood, H. (2011). Effects of written emotional disclosure on implicit self-esteem and body image. *British Journal of Health Psychology, 16*(3), 488-501.

O'Connor, D. B., Walker, S., Hendrickx, H., Talbot, D., & Schaefer, A. (2012). Stress-related thinking predicts the cortisol awakening response and somatic symptoms in healthy adults. *Psychoneuroendocrinology. 38*(3):438-446.

Opre, A., Coman, A., Kallay, E., Rotaru, D., & Manier, D. (2005). Reducing distress in college students through expressive writing: A pilot study on a Romanian sample. *Cogniie, Creier, &Comportament [Cognition, Brain, & Behavior], 10*, 53-64.

Owen, J. E., Hanson, E. R., Preddy, D. A., & Bantum, E. O. C. (2011). Linguistically-tailored video feedback increases total and positive emotional expression in a structured writing task. *Computers in Human Behavior, 27*(2), 874-882.

Pachankis, J. E., & Goldfried, M. R. (2010). Expressive writing for gay-related stress: psychosocial benefits and mechanisms underlying improvement. *Journal of Consultative Clinical Psychology, 78*(1), 98-110.

Pachankis, J. E., & Goldfried, M. R. (2010). Expressive writing for gay-related stress: Psychosocial benefits and mechanisms underlying improvement. *Journal of Consulting and Clinical Psychology, 78*(1), 98.

Paez, D., Velasco, C., & Gonzalez, J. L. (1999). Expressive writing and the role of alexithymia as a dispositional deficit in self-disclosure and psychological health. *Journal of Personality and Social Psychology, 77*, 630-641.

Palmer, G., & Braud, W. (2002). Exceptional human experiences, disclosure, and a more inclusive view of physical, psychological, and spiritual well-being. *The Journal of Transpersonal Psychology, 34*, 29-61.

Pantchenko, T., Lawson, M., & Joyce, M. R. (2003). Verbal and non-verbal disclosure of recalled and negative experiences: Relation to well-being. *Psychology and Psychotherapy: Theory, Research, and Practice, 76*, 251-265.

Park, C. L. (2010). Making sense of the meaning literature: an integrative review of meaning making and its effects on adjustment to stressful life events. *Psychological Bulletin, 136*(2), 257.

Park, C. L. & Blumberg, C. J. (2002). Disclosing trauma through writing: Testing the meaning-making hypothesis. *Cognitive Therapy and Research, 26*, 597-616.

Park, E. Y., & Yi, M. (2012). Development and effectiveness of expressive writing program for women with breast cancer in Korea. *Journal of Korean Academy of Nursing, 42*(2), 269-279.

Patterson, C. L., & Singer, J. A. (2007-2008). Exploring the role of expectancies in the mental and physical health outcomes of written self-disclosure. *Imagination, Cognition and Personality, 27*, 99-115.

Pauley, P. M., Morman, M. T., & Floyd, K. (2011). Expressive writing improves subjective health among testicular cancer survivors: A pilot study. *International Journal of Men's Health, 10*(3), 199-219.

Peeler, S., Chung, M. C., Stedmon, J., & Skirton, H. (2013). A review assessing the current treatment strategies for postnatal psychological morbidity with a focus on post-traumatic stress disorder. *Midwifery, 29*(4), 377-388.

Pennebaker, J. W., Barger, S. D., & Tiebout, J. (1989). Disclosure of traumas and health among Holocaust survivors. *Psychosomatic Medicine, 51*, 577-589.

Pennebaker, J. W., & Beall, S. K. (1986). Confronting a traumatic event: Toward an understanding of inhibition and disease. *Journal of Abnormal Psychology, 95*, 274-281.

Pennebaker, J. W., & Chung, C. K. (2011). Expressive writing: Connections to physical and mental health. *Oxford Handbook of Health Psychology*, 417-437. ed H. S. Friedman. Oxford" Oxford University Press.

Pennebaker, J. W., Colder, M., & Sharp, L. K. (1990). Accelerating the coping process. *Journal of Personality and Social Psychology, 58*, 528-537.

Pennebaker, J. W., & Francis, M. E. (1996). Cognitive, emotional, and language processes in disclosure. *Cognition and Emotion, 10*, 601-626.

Pennebaker, J. W., & Graybeal, A. (2001). Patterns of natural language use: Disclosure, personality, and social integration. *Current Directions in Psychological Science, 10*, 90-93.

Pennebaker, J. W., Hughes, C. F. & O'Heeron, R. C. (1987). The psychophysiology of confession: Linking inhibitory and psychosomatic processes. *Journal of Personality and Social Psychology, 52*, 781-793.

Pennebaker, J. W., Kiecolt-Glaser, J. K., & Glaser, R. (1988). Disclosure of traumas and immune function: health implications for psychotherapy. *Journal of Consulting and Clinical Psychology, 56*, 239-245.

Pennebaker, J. W., Mayne, T. J., & Francis, M. E. (1997). Linguistic predictors of adaptive bereavement. *Journal of Personality and Social Psychology, 72*, 863-871.

Pennebaker, J. W., Mehl, M. R., & Niederhoffer, K. G. (in press). Psychological aspects of natural language use: Our words, our selves. *Annual Review of Psychology.*

Pennebaker, J. W., & Susman, J. R. (1988). Disclosure of traumas and psychosomatic processes. *Social Science and Medicine, 26*, 327-332.

Petrie, K. J., Booth, R., Pennebaker, J. W., Davison, K. P., & Thomas, M. (1995). Disclosure of trauma and immune response to Hepatitis B vaccination program. *Journal of Consulting and Clinical Psychology, 63*, 787-792.

Petrie, K. J., Fontanilla, I., Thomas, M. G., Booth, R. J., & Pennebaker. J. W. (2004). Effect of written emotional expression on immune function in patients with HIV infection: A randomized trial. *Psychosomatic Medicine, 66*, 272-275.

Petrie, K. P., Booth, R. J., & Pennebaker, J. W. (1998). The immunological effects of thought suppression. *Journal of Personality and Social Psychology, 75*, 1264-1272.

Pinhasi-Vittorio, L. (2007). The role of written language in the rehabilitation process of brain injury and aphasia: the memory of the movement in the reacquisition of language. *Top Stroke Rehabilitation, 14*(1), 115-122.

Pinhasi-Vittorio, L. (2008). Poetry and prose in the self-perception of one man who lives with brain injury and aphasia. *Top Stroke Rehabilitation, 15*(3), 288-294.

Pini, S., Harley, C., O'Connor, D., & Velikova, G. (2011). Evaluation of expressive writing as an intervention for patients following a mastectomy for breast cancer — a feasibility study. *BMJ Supportive & Palliative Care, 1*(Suppl 1), A24-A24.

Pizarro, J. (2004). The efficacy of art and writing therapy: Increasing positive mental health outcomes and participant retention after exposure to traumatic experience. *Art Therapy, 21*, 5-12.

Poon, A., & Danoff-Burg, S. (2011). Mindfulness as a moderator in expressive writing. *Journal of Clinical Psychology, 67*(9), 881-895.

Possemato, K., Ouimette, P., & Geller, P. A. (2010). Internet-based expressive writing for kidney transplant recipients: Effects on posttraumatic stress and quality of life. *Traumatology, 16*(1), 49-54.

Radcliffe, A. M., Lumley, M. A., Kendall, J., Stevenson, J. K., & Beltran, J. (2010). Written emotional disclosure: Testing whether social disclosure matters. *Journal of social and clinical psychology, 26*(3), 362.

Radcliffe, A. M., Stevenson, J. K., Lumley, M. A., D'Souza, P. J., & Kraft, C. A. (2010). Does written emotional disclosure about stress improve college students' academic Performance? results from three randomized, controlled studies. *Journal of College Student Retention: Research, Theory and Practice, 12*(4), 407-428.

Ramirez, G., & Beilock, S. L. (2011). Writing about testing worries boosts exam performance in the classroom. *Science, 331*(6014), 211-213.

Range, L. M., & Jenkins, S. R. (2010). Who benefits from Pennebaker's expressive writing paradigm? Research recommendations from three gender theories. *Sex Roles, 63*(3-4), 149-164.

Range, L. M., Kovac, S. H., & Marion, M. S. (2000). Does writing about the bereavement lessen grief following sudden, unintentional death? *Death Studies, 24*, 115-134.

Re, A. M., Caeran, M., & Cornoldi, C. (2008). Improving expressive writing skills of children rated for ADHD symptoms. *Journal of Learning Disabilities, 41*(6), 535-544.

Re, A. M., & Cornoldi, C. (2010). ADHD expressive writing difficulties of ADHD children: when good declarative knowledge is not sufficient. *European Journal of Psychology of Education, 25*(3), 315-323.

Re, A. M., Pedron, M., & Cornoldi, C. (2007). Expressive writing difficulties in children described as exhibiting ADHD symptoms. *Journal of Learning Disabilities, 40*(3), 244-55.

Ressler, P. K., Bradshaw, Y. S., Gualtieri, L., & Chui, K. K. H. (2012). Communicating the experience of chronic pain and illness through blogging. *Journal of Medical Internet Research, 14*(5).

Reynolds, M., Brewin, C. R., & Saxton, M. (2000). Emotional disclosure in school children. *Journal of Child Psychology & Psychiatry & Allied Disciplines, 41*, 151-159.

Richards, J. M., Beal, W. E., Seagal, J., & Pennebaker, J. W. (2000). The effects of disclosure of traumatic events on illness behavior among psychiatric prison inmates. *Journal of Abnormal Psychology, 109*, 156-160.

Rickwood, D., & Bradford, S. (2012). The role of self-help in the treatment of mild anxiety disorders in young people: an evidence-based review. *Psychology Research and Behavior Management, 5*, 25.

Rimé, B. (1995). Mental rumination, social sharing, and the recovery from emotional exposure. In *Emotion, Disclosure, and Health,* edited by J. W. Pennebaker, 271-291. Washington, DC: American Psychological Association.

Rivkin, I. D., Gustafson, J., Weingarten, I., & Chin, D. (2006). The effects of expressive writing on adjustment to HIV. *AIDS Behavior, 10*(1), 13-26.

Rooke, S. E., & Malouff, J. M. (in press). The efficacy of symbolic modeling and vicarious reinforcement in increasing coping-method adherence. *Behavior Therapy.*

Rosenberg, MA, H. J., Rosenberg, Ph. D, S. D., Ernstoff, MD, M. S., Wolford, Ph. D, G. I., Amdur, MD, R. J., Elshamy, AMP, M. R., ... & Pennebaker, Ph. D, J. W. (2002). Expressive disclosure and health outcomes in a prostate cancer population. *International Journal of Psychiatry in Medicine, 32*(1), 37-53.

Rubin, D. C., Boals, A., & Klein, K. (2010). Autobiographical memories for very negative events: the effects of thinking about and rating memories. *Cognition Therapy Research, 34*(1), 35-48.

Rye, M. S., Fleri, A. M., Moore, C. D., Worthington Jr., E. L., Wade, N. G., Sandage, S. J., & Cook, K. M. (2012). Evaluation of an intervention designed to help divorced parents forgive their ex-spouse. *Journal of Divorce & Remarriage, 53*(3), 231-245.

Sandgren, A. K., & McCaul, K. D. (2003). Short-term effects of telephone therapy for breast cancer patients. *Health Psychology, 22*, 310-315.

Sbarra, D. A., Boals, A., Mason, A. E., Larson, G. M., & Mehl, M. R. (2013). Expressive writing can impede emotional recovery following marital separation. *Clinical Psychological Science, 1*(2): 120-134.

Schilte, A. F., Portegijs, P. J. M., Blankenstein, A. H., van der Horst, H. E., Latour, M. B. F., van Eijk, J. T. M., & Knottnerus, J. A. (2001). Randomised controlled trial of disclosure of emotionally important events in somatisation in primary care. *British Medical Journal, 323*, 86.

Schoutrop, M. J. A., Lange, A., Brosschot, J., & Everaerd, W. (1997). Overcoming traumatic events by means of writing assignments. In *The (Non)Expression of Emotions in Health and Disease,* edited by A. Vingerhoets, F. van Bussel, & J. Boelhouwer, 279-289. Tilburg, The Netherlands: Tilburg University Press.

Schoutroup, M. J. A., Brosschot, J. F, & Lange, A. (1999). Writing assignments after trauma: decreased re-experiencing and within/across session physiological habituation [abstract]. *Psychosomatic Medicine, 61*, 95.

Schoutrop, M. J. A., Lange, A., Hanewald, G., Davidovich, U., & Salomon, H. (2002). Structured writing and processing major stressful events: A controlled trial. *Psychotherapy and Psychosomatics, 71*, 141-157.

Schut, H. A. W., Stroebe, M. S., & van den Bout, J. (1997). Intervention for the bereaved: Gender differences in the efficacy of two counselling programmes. *British Journal of Clinical Psychology, 36,*63-72.

Schutte, N. S., Searle, T., Meade, S., & Dark, N. A. (2012). The effect of meaningfulness and integrative processing in expressive writing on positive and negative affect and life satisfaction. *Cognition and Emotion, 26*(1), 144-152.

Schwartz, L., & Drotar, D. (2004). Effects of written emotional disclosure on caregivers of children and adolescents with chronic illness. *Journal of Pediatric Psychology, 29*, 105-118.

Scott, V. B., Robare, R. D., Raines, D. B., Konwinski, S. J. M., Chanin, J. A., & Tolley, R. S. (2003). Emotive writing moderates the relationship between mood awareness and athletic performance in collegiate tennis players. *North American Journal of Psychology, 5*, 311-324

Segal, D. L. & Murray, E. J. (1994). Emotional processing in cognitive therapy and vocal expression of feeling. *Journal of Social and Clinical Psychology, 13*, 189-206.

Segal, D. L., & Murray, E. J. (2001). Comparison of distance emotional expression with psychotherapy. In *Distance Writing and Computer-Assisted Techniques in Psychiatry and Mental Health,* edited by L. L'Abate, 61-75. Greenwich, CT: Ablex.

Segal, D. L., Bogaards, J. A., Becker, L. A., & Chatman, C. (1999). Effects of emotional expression on adjustment to spousal loss among older adults. *Journal of Mental Health and Aging, 5*, 297-310.

Segal, D. L., Chatman, C., Bogaards, J. A., & Becker, L. A. (2001). One year follow-up of an emotional expression intervention for bereaved older adults. *Journal of Mental Health and Aging, 7*, 465-472.

Segal, D. L., Tucker, H. C., & Coolidge, F. L. (2009). A comparison of positive versus negative emotional expression in a written disclosure study among distressed students. *Journal of Aggression, Maltreatment & Trauma, 18*, 367-381.

Seih, Y. T., Chung, C. K., & Pennebaker, J. W. (2011). Experimental manipulations of perspective taking and perspective switching in expressive writing. *Cognition and Emotion, 25*(5), 926-938.

Seih, Y. T., Lin, Y. C., Huang, C. L., Peng, C. W., & Huang, S. P. (2008). The benefits of psychological displacement in diary writing when using different pronouns. *British Journal of Health Psychology, 13*, 39-41.

Seligman, M. E. (2011). *Learned optimism: How to change your mind and your life.* New York: Vintage.

Seligman, M. E. (2012). *Flourish: A visionary new understanding of happiness and well-being.* New York: Simon and Schuster.

Seligman, M. E., & Csikszentmihalyi, M. (2000). Positive psychology. *The science of optimism and hope: Research essays in honor of Martin EP Seligman*, 415-429.

Sharifabad, M. A., Hurewitz, A., Spiegler, P., Bernstein, M., Feuerman, M., & Smyth, J. M. (2010). Written disclosure therapy for patients with chronic lung disease undergoing pulmonary rehabilitation. *Journal of Cardiopulmonary Rehabilitation and Prevention, 30*(5), 340-345.

Sharma-Patel, K., Brown, E. J., & Chaplin, W. F. (2012). Emotional and cognitive processing in sexual assault survivors' narratives. *Journal of Aggression, Maltreatment & Trauma, 21*(2), 149-170.

Sheese, B. E., Brown, E. L., & Graziano, W. G. (2004). Emotional expression in cyberspace: Searching for moderators of the Pennebaker disclosure effect via email. *Health Psychology, 23*, 457-464.

Sheffield, D., Duncan, E., Thomson, K., Johal, S. S. (2002). Written emotional expression and well-being: Result from a home-based study. *The Australasian Journal of Disaster and Trauma Studies, 2001.* Retrieved May 21, 2004, from http://www.massey.ac.nz/~trauma/issues/2002-1/sheffield.htm

Shim, M., Cappella, J. N., & Han, J. Y. (2011). How does insightful and emotional disclosure bring potential health benefits? Study based on online support groups for women with breast cancer. *Journal of Communication, 61*(3), 432-454.

Shnabel, N., Purdie-Vaughns, V., Cook, J. E., Garcia, J., & Cohen, G. L. (2013). Demystifying values-affirmation interventions writing about social belonging is a key to buffering against identity threat. *Personality and Social Psychology Bulletin, 39*(5), 663-676.

Silvia, P. J., & Duval, T. S. (2001). Objective self-awareness theory: Recent progress and enduring problems. *Personality and Social Psychology Review, 5,* 230-241.

Sklar, E. R., & Carty, J. N. (2012). Emotional disclosure interventions for chronic pain: from the laboratory to the clinic. *Translational Behavioral Medicine, 2*(1), 73-81.

Slatcher, R. B., & Pennebaker, J. W. (2006). How do I love thee? Let me count the words: the social effects of expressive writing. *Psychology Science, 17*(8), 660-664.

Slatcher, R. B., Robles, T. F., Repetti, R. L., & Fellows, M. D. (2010). Momentary work worries, marital disclosure, and salivary cortisol among parents of young children. *Psychosomatic Medicine, 72*(9), 887-896.

Slavin-Spenny, O. M., Cohen, J. L., Oberleitner, L. M., & Lumley, M. A. (2011). The effects of different methods of emotional disclosure: differentiating post-traumatic growth from stress symptoms. *Journal of Clinical Psychology, 67*(10), 993-1007.

Sloan, D. M., & Epstein, E. M. (2005). Respiratory sinus arrhythmia predicts written disclosure outcome. *Psychophysiology, 42*, 611-615.

Sloan, D. M., & Marx, B. P. (2004). A closer examination of the structured written disclosure procedure. *Journal of Consulting and Clinical Psychology, 72*, 165-175.

Sloan, D. M., & Marx, B. P. (2004). Taking pen to hand: Evaluating theories underlying the written disclosure paradigm. *Clinical Psychology: Science and Practice, 11*, 121-137.

Sloan, D. M., Feinstein, B. A., & Marx, B. P. (2009). The durability of beneficial health effects associated with expressive writing. *Anxiety Stress Coping, 22*(5), 509-523.

Sloan, D. M., Marx, B. P., & Epstein, E. M. (2005). Further examination of the exposure model underlying the efficacy of written emotional disclosure. *Journal of Consulting and Clinical Psychology, 73*, 549-554.

Sloan, D. M., Marx, B. P., Epstein, E. M., & Dobbs, J. L. (2008). Expressive writing buffers against maladaptive rumination. *Emotion, 8*(2), 302-306.

Sloan, D. M., Marx, B. P., Epstein, E. M., & Lexington, J. (in press). Does altering the writing instructions influence outcome associated with written disclosure? *Behavior Therapy*.

Small, R., Lumley, J., Donohue, L., Potter, A., & Waldenstrom, U. (2000). Randomised controlled trial of midwife led debriefing to reduce maternal depression after childbirth. *British Medical Journal, 321*, 1043-1047.

Smith, H. E., Jones, C. J., Theasom, A., Horne, R., Bowskill, R., Nakins, M., & Frew, A. J. (2009). Writing about emotional experiences reduces B-agonist use in patients with asthma — 3-month follow up of a randomized controlled trial. *The Journal of Allergy and Clinical Immunology, 123*, S80. doi:10.1016/j.jaci.2008.12.280

Smith, S., Anderson-Hanley, C., Langrock, A., & Compas, B. (2005). The effects of journaling for women with newly diagnosed breast cancer. *Psycho-oncology, 14*(12), 1075-1082.

Smyth, J. M. (1998). Written emotional expression: Effect sizes, outcome types, and moderating variables. *Journal of Consulting and Clinical Psychology, 66*, 174-184.

Smyth, J. M., & Arigo, D. (2009). Recent evidence supports emotion-regulation interventions for improving health in at-risk and clinical populations. *Current Opinion in Psychiatry, 22*(2), 205-210.

Smyth, J. M., & Pennebaker, J. W. (2008). Exploring the boundary conditions of expressive writing: in search of the right recipe. *British Journal of Health Psychology, 13*(Pt 1), 1-7.

Smyth, J. M., Hockemeyer, J. R., & Tulloch, H. (2008). Expressive writing and post-traumatic stress disorder: effects on trauma symptoms, mood states, and cortisol reactivity. *British Journal of Health Psychology, 13*(Pt 1), 85-93.

Smyth, J. M., Hockemeyer, J., Anderson, C., Strandberg, K., Koch, M., O'Neill, H. K., et al. (2002). Structured writing about a natural disaster buffers the effect of intrusive thoughts on negative affect and physical symptoms. *The Australasian Journal of Disaster, 2002*. Retrieved May 21, 2004 from http://www.massey.ac.nz/~trauma/issues/2002-1/smyth.htm

Smyth, J. M., Stone, A. A., Hurewitz, A., & Kaell, A. (1999). Effects of writing about stressful experiences on symptom reduction in patients with asthma or rheumatoid arthritis: a randomized trial. *Journal of American Medical Association, 281*, 1304-1309.

Smyth, J., Anderson, C., Hockemeyer, J., & Stone, A. (in press). Emotional non-expression, cognitive avoidance, and response to writing about traumatic events. *Psychology & Health*.

Smyth, J., True, N., & Souto, J. (2001). Effects of writing about traumatic experiences: The necessity for narrative structure. *Journal of Social & Clinical Psychology, 20*, 161-172.

Smyth, J. M. (1998). Written emotional expression: Effect sizes, outcome types, and moderating variables. *Journal of Consulting & Clinical Psychology, 66*, 174-184.

Snyder, D. K., Gordon, K. C., & Baucom, D. H. (2004). Treating affair couples: Extending the written disclosure paradigm to relationship trauma. *Clinical Psychology: Science and Practice, 11*(2), 155-159.

Solano, L., Donati, V., Pecci, F., Persichetti, S., & Colaci, A. (2003). Post-operative course after papilloma resection: effects of written disclosure of the experience in subjects with different alexithymia levels. *Psychosomatic Medicine, 65,* 477-484.

Soliday, E., Garofalo, J. P., & Rogers, D. (2004). Expressive writing intervention for adolescents' somatic symptoms and mood. *Journal of Clinical Child Adolescent Psychology, 33*(4), 792-801.

Spera, S. P., Buhrfeind, E. D., & Pennebaker, J. W. (1994). Expressive writing and coping with job loss. *Academy of Management Journal, 37,* 722-733.

Stanton, A. L., & Low, C. A. (2012). Expressing Emotions in Stressful Contexts Benefits, Moderators, and Mechanisms. *Current Directions in Psychological Science, 21*(2), 124-128.

Stanton, A. L., Danoff-Burg, S., Cameron, C. L., Bishop, M., Collins, C. A., Kirk, S. B., Sworowski, L. A., & Twillman, R. (2000). Emotionally expressive coping predicts psychological and physical adjustment to breast cancer. *Journal of Consulting and Clinical Psychology, 68,* 875-882.

Stanton, A. L., Danoff-Burg, S., Sworowski, L. A., Collins, C. A., Branstetter, A. D., Rodriguez-Hanley, A., Kirk, S. B., & Austenfeld, J. L. (2002). Randomized, controlled trial of written emotional expression and benefit finding in breast cancer patients. *Journal of Clinical Oncology, 20,* 4160-4168.

Stice, E., Rohde, P., Gau, J., & Shaw, H. (2012). Effect of a dissonance-based prevention program on risk for eating disorder onset in the context of eating disorder risk factors. *Prevention Science, 13*(2), 129-139.

Stickney, L. T. (2010). Who benefits from Pennebaker's expressive writing? More research recommendations: a commentary on range and Jenkins. *Sex Roles, 63*(3-4), 165-172.

Stockdale, B. (2011). Writing in physical and concomitant mental illness: biological underpinnings and applications for practice. In *Research on Writing Approaches in Mental Health*, edited by L. L'Abate & L. Sweeny, 23-35. United Kingdom: Emerald.

Stone, A., Smyth, J., Kaell, A., & Hurewitz, A. (2000). Structured writing about stressful events: Exploring potential psychological mediators of positive health effects. *Health Psychology, 19,* 619-624.

Stroebe, M., Stroebe, W., Zech, E., & Schut, H. (2002). Does disclosure of emotions facilitate recovery from bereavement? Evidence from two prospective studies. *Journal of Consulting and Clinical Psychology, 70,* 169-178.

Swanbon, T., Boyce, L., & Greenberg, M. A. (2008). Expressive writing reduces avoidance and somatic complaints in a community sample with constraints on expression. *British Journal of Health Psychology, 13*(Pt 1), 53-56.

Tamagawa, R., Moss-Morris, R., Martin, A., Robinson, E., & Booth, R. J. (2012). Dispositional emotion coping styles and physiological responses to expressive writing. *British Journal of Health Psychology.*

Tavakoli, S., Lumley, M. A., Hijazi, A. M., Slavin-Spenny, O. M., & Parris, G. P. (2009). Effects of assertiveness training and expressive writing on acculturative stress in international students: a randomized trial. *Journal of Counseling Psychology, 56*(4), 590-596.

Taylor, L.A., Wallander, J. L., & Anderson, D. (2003). Improving health care utilization, improving chronic disease utilization, health status, and adjustment in adolescents and young adults with cystic fibrosis: A preliminary report. *Journal of Clinical Psychology in Medical Settings, 10,* 9-16.

Toepfer, S. M., Cichy, K., & Peters, P. (2012). Letters of gratitude: further evidence for author benefits. *Journal of Happiness Studies, 13*(1), 187-201.

Trees, A. R., Kellas, J. K., & Roche, M. (2010). Family narratives. *Family communication about genetics: Theory and practice,* 68-86.

Troop, N. A., Chilcot, J., Hutchings, L., & Varnaite, G. (2012). Expressive writing, self-criticism, and self-assurance. *Psychology and Psychotherapy: Theory, Research, and Practice*, DOI:10.1111/j.2044-8341.2012.02065.x.

Ullman, S. E. (2011). Is disclosure of sexual traumas helpful? Comparing experimental laboratory versus field study results. *Journal of Aggression, Maltreatment & Trauma, 20*(2), 148-162.

Ullrich, P. A. & Lutgendorf, S. L. (2002). Journaling about stressful events: Effects of cognitive processing and emotional expression. *Annals of Behavioral Medicine, 24*, 244-250.

Unsworth, K. L., Rogelberg, S. G., & Bonilla, D. (2010). Emotional expressive writing to alleviate euthanasia-related stress. *Canadian Veterinary Journal, 51*(7), 775-777.

van der Houwen, K., Schut, H., van den Bout, J., Stroebe, M., & Stroebe, W. (2010). The efficacy of a brief internet-based self-help intervention for the bereaved. *Behaviour Research and Therapy, 48*(5), 359-367.

Van Dijk, J. A., Schoutrop, M. J. A., Spinhoven, P. (2003). Testimony therapy: Treatment method for traumatized victims of organized violence. *American Journal of Psychotherapy, 57*, 361-373.

van Emmerik, A. A. P., K., Kamphuis, J. H., & Emmelkamp, P. M. G. (2008). Treating acute stress disorder and post-traumatic stress disorder with cognitive behavioral therapy or structured writing therapy: A randomized controlled trial. *Psychotherapy and Psychosomatics, 77*, 93-100.

Viel-Ruma, K., Houchins, D. E., Jolivette, K., Fredrick, L. D., & Gama, R. (2010). Direct instruction in written expression: The effects on English speakers and English language learners with disabilities. *Learning Disabilities Research & Practice, 25*(2), 97-108.

Vrielynck, N., Philippot, P., & Rime, B. (2010). Level of processing modulates benefits of writing about stressful events: Comparing generic and specific recall. *Cognition & Emotion, 24*, 1117-1132. http://dx.doi.org/10.1080/ 02699930903172161.

Wagner, L. J., Hilker, K. A., Hepworth, J. T., & Wallston, K. A. (2010). Cognitive adaptability as a moderator of expressive writing effects in an HIV sample. *AIDS Behavior, 14*(2), 410-420.

Walker, B. L., Nail, L. M., & Croyle, R. T. (1999). Does emotional expression make a difference in reactions to breast cancer? *Oncology Nursing Forum, 26*, 1025-1032.

Wallander, J. L., Madan-Swain, A., Klapow, J., & Saeed, S. (2011). A randomised controlled trial of written self-disclosure for functional recurrent abdominal pain in youth. *Psychology and Health, 26*(4), 433-447.

Warner, L. J., Lumley, M. A., Casey, R. J., Pierantoni, W., Salazar, R., Zoratti, E. M., Enberg, R., & Simon, M. R. (2006). Health effects of written emotional disclosure in adolescents with asthma: A randomized, controlled trial. *Journal of Pediatric Psychology, 31*, 557-568.

Waters, T. E., Shallcross, J. F., & Fivush, R. (2013). The many facets of meaning making: Comparing multiple measures of meaning making and their relations to psychological distress. *Memory, 21*(1), 111-124.

Wegner, D. M. (2002). *The illusion of conscious will*. Cambridge, MA: MIT Press.

Weine, S. M., Kulenovic, A. D., Pavkovic, I., Gibbons, R. (1998). Testimony psychotherapy in Bosnian refugees: A pilot study. *American Journal of Psychiatry, 155*, 1720-1726.

Wetherell, M.A., Byrne-Davis, L., Dieppe, P., et al. (2005). Effects of emotional disclosure on psychological and physiological outcomes in patients with rheumatoid arthritis: An exploratory home-based study. *Journal of Health Psychology, 10*, 277-285.

Wicklund, R. A. (1979). The influence of self-awareness on human behavior: The person who becomes self-aware is more likely to act consistently, be faithful to societal norms, and give accurate reports about himself. *American Scientist, 67*(2), 187-193.

Williams, C., & Pilonieta, P. (2012). Using interactive writing instruction with kindergarten and first-grade English language learners. *Early Childhood Education Journal, 40*(3), 145-150.

Willmott, L., Harris, P., Gellaitry, G., Cooper, V., & Horne, R. (2011). The effects of expressive writing following first myocardial infarction: A randomized controlled trial. *Health Psychology, 30*(5), 642-650.

Wolbers, K. A., Dostal, H. M., & Bowers, L. M. (2012). "I was born full deaf." Written language outcomes after 1 year of strategic and interactive writing instruction. *Journal of Deaf Studies and Deaf Education, 17*(1), 19-38.

Wolitzky-Taylor, K. B., & Telch, M. J. (2010). Efficacy of self-administered treatments for pathological academic worry: a randomized controlled trial. *Behavioral Research Therapy, 48*(9), 840-850.

Wong, Y. J., & Rochlen, A. B. (2009). Potential benefits of expressive writing for male college students with varying degrees of restrictive emotionality. *Psychology of Men & Masculinity, 10,* 149-159.

Wortman, C. B., & Silver, R. C. (1989). The myths of coping with loss. *Journal of Consulting and Clinical Psychology, 57,* 349-357.

Wright, J. K. (2003) Five women talk about work-related brief therapy and therapeutic writing. *Counselling and Psychotherapy Research, 3,* 204-209.

Wright, J. K. (2005) Writing therapy in brief workplace counselling, *Counselling and Psychotherapy Research, 5,* 111-119.

Yogo, M., & Fujihara, S. (2008). Working memory capacity can be improved by expressive writing: a randomized experiment in a Japanese sample. *British Journal of Health Psychology, 13*(Pt 1), 77-80.

Zakowski, S. G., Herzer, M., Barrett, S. D., Milligan, J. G., & Beckman, N. (2011). Who benefits from emotional expression? An examination of personality differences among gynaecological cancer patients participating in a randomized controlled emotional disclosure intervention trial. *British Journal of Psychology, 102*(3), 355-372.

Zakowski, S. G., Ramati, A., Morton, C., Johnson, P., & Flanigan, R. (2004). Written emotional disclosure buffers the effects of social constraints on distress in cancer patients. *Health Psychology, 23,*555-563.

Zuuren, F. J. van, Schoutrop, M. J. A., Lange, A., Louis, C. M., & Slegers, J. E. M. (1999). Effective and ineffective ways of writing about traumatic experiences: a qualitative study. *Psychotherapy Research, 9,* 363-380.

Photo Credits

	<a href='http://www.123rf.com/photo_10888070_fountain-luxury-pen-with-written-trace-on-white.html'>coliap / 123RF Stock Photo</a>
	<a href='http://www.123rf.com/photo_19608354_young-female-is-writing-notes-and-planning-her-schedule.html'>petro / 123RF Stock Photo</a>
	<a href='http://www.123rf.com/photo_17234466_notebook-and-pen-and-tablet-on-white-background.html'>daniilantiq / 123RF Stock Photo</a>
	<a href='http://www.123rf.com/photo_14386525_female-hands-typing-on-white-computer-keyboard.html'>yanlev / 123RF Stock Photo</a>
	<a href='http://www.123rf.com/photo_9979420_reading-glasses-and-a-ballpoint-pen-lie-on-a-newspaper.html'>rrrneumi / 123RF Stock Photo</a>
	<a href='http://www.123rf.com/photo_13501496_a-vintage-fountain-pen-leaning-against-an-open-bottle-of-ink.html'>leeavison / 123RF Stock Photo</a>
	<a href='http://www.123rf.com/photo_12093457_hand-with-pen.html'>thirteenfifty / 123RF Stock Photo</a>
	<a href='http://www.123rf.com/photo_20075072_picture-of-businessman-writing-something-on-the-paper.html'>dolgachov / 123RF Stock Photo</a>
	<a href='http://www.123rf.com/photo_9767351_portable-electronic-book-lying-on-the-grass.html'>bloomua / 123RF Stock Photo</a>
	<a href='http://www.123rf.com/photo_17718116_young-woman-student-learning-in-the-nature.html'>menuha / 123RF Stock Photo</a>
	<a href='http://www.123rf.com/photo_19716390_pen.html'>magurok / 123RF Stock Photo</a>
	<a href='http://www.123rf.com/photo_11575070_doodle-style-feather-quill-pen-and-ink-well-illustration-in-vector-format.html'>lhfgraphics / 123RF Stock Photo</a>
	<a href='http://www.123rf.com/photo_17640001_close-up-image-of-a-business-woman-being-to-put-her-signature.html'>pressmaster / 123RF Stock Photo</a>
	<a href='http://www.123rf.com/photo_15705077_tablet-computer-and-laptop-pen-and-paper-notebook.html'>petro / 123RF Stock Photo</a>